Lincoln College - Oxford
19 Oct. 1901

Mr. Mohamed Ali joined this College after a successful career at the University of Allahabad.

His conduct has been altogether satisfactory, and he shows himself to be of active mind, literary interests, & high ambitions.

His Tutors report to me their appreciation of his ability and intelligence; and I think him very well fitted for doing good work in an educational post in India, which is the career which he desires.

W W Merry D.D.
Rector of Lincoln College

MOHAMED ALI
IDEOLOGY AND POLITICS

Mohamed Ali
Ideology and Politics

MUSHIRUL HASAN

MANOHAR
2020

First published 1981
Reprinted 2020

ISBN 978-81-943521-7-4

Published by
Ajay Kumar Jain *for*
Manohar Publishers & Distributors
4753/23 Ansari Road, Daryaganj
New Delhi 110 002

Printed at
Replika Press Pvt. Ltd.

To
Salma, Mujib, Sonny and Najju

CONTENTS

LIST OF PLATES

[pp. 57-64]

PREFACE

This study attempts to give a brief description of Mohamed Ali's ideology and thought in a relatively short compass. It begins with a biographical sketch, continues with chapters on Mohamed Ali's association with and involvement in various religious and political movements, and concludes with an assessment that aims to delineate the many strands in his ideological make-up. The Appendices contain some hitherto unpublished correspondence of Mohamed Ali. They are drawn from sources in India, Pakistan and England.

In dealing with certain aspects of Indian politics in the 1920s, I have drawn freely upon my book, *Nationalism and Communal Politics in India, 1916-1928*, published in 1979. I apologise to those of my readers who have read the earlier book, but it seemed to me unnecessary to go to the labour of rewriting what I had already expressed as well and clearly as I could.

The actual writing of this book has not occupied me for very long, but the subject has furnished the theme of constant discussion with friends and acquaintances for many years. I take this opportunity of thanking them all. In particular, I would like to mention the names of Francis Robinson, Prabhat Patnaik, Christopher Bayly, Majid Hayat Siddiqi, Satish Saberwal, Simon Commander, Atiq Siddiqi. My father, Mohibbul Hasan, and Mr. Anwar Jamal Kidwai, Vice-Chancellor, Jamia Millia Islamia, have been a source of great help and encouragement.

I am grateful to Khalid S. Hasan for generously devoting his time and energy to my problems in Pakistan; to Reva Pathak for her kind assistance in helping with the research materials; to Naziruddin Meenai and Azizuddin Husain for their help in translating some Urdu materials; to the librarians and staff of Zakir Husain Library, Jamia Millia Islamia, and the Nehru Memorial

Museum and Library for their kind and courteous help; to Zoya and Abdur Rashid for reading the manuscript and much improving its style; to my senior colleagues, M.A. Ansari, S.N. Sinha and R.A. Khan, for their encouragement during the making of this book; to Aqeela, Hamida, Tipu, Kahkashan, and Saman for their hospitality during my stay in Jamia Nagar this summer.

In the preparation of this volume I have benefited from the courtesy and expertise of Mr. K.K. Paulose and the staff of Printaid.

My thanks are again due to Mr. Shabih Haider Rizvi who patiently bore the burden of typing and retyping the manuscript of this book and helping me to prepare it for publication.

Department of History and Culture MUSHIRUL HASAN
Jamia Millia Islamia
New Delhi-110025
August 1981

ABBREVIATIONS

AMUA	Aligarh Muslim University Archives, Aligarh.
CUL	Cambridge University Library.
CWG	The Collected Works of M.K. Gandhi.
D	Deposit.
EUR	European.
FR	Fortnightly Report.
IOL	India Office Library, London.
JMI	Jamia Millia Islamia, Delhi.
M.A.O.	Muhammadan Anglo-Oriental College, Aligarh.
MAP	Mohamed Ali Papers.
MSS	Manuscript.
NAI	National Archives of India, Delhi.
NML	Nehru Memorial Museum and Library, Delhi.
Poll.	Political.
UP	United Provinces of Agra and Oudh.
WR	Weekly Report.
WRDCI	Weekly Report of the Director of Central Intelligence.

INTRODUCTION

Mohamed Ali was a figure of stormy dispute for his contemporaries and for posterity. Government officials associated him with the 'extreme faction of the Muslim community', the 'Advanced Party' and the 'hot headed Nationalist Party'.[1] Fed with exaggerated reports of a Turko-German conspiracy to incite the Indian Muslims against the British government, they recognised Mohamed Ali as leader of the pan-Islamic group, 'a clique of noisy and aggressive Muslims of the young party, who make the Raja's house (Raja of Mahmudabad) their headquarters and live and agitate at his expense'.[2] James Meston, in particular, regarded Mohamed Ali as the ideological stormtrooper of the pan-Islamic bogey and the chief architect of the Congress-Muslim League alliance. He lamented the fact that a 'mischievous agitator' like Mohamed Ali not only weilded considerable influence amongst Muslims, but also humbled his pro-government opponents so decisively. In a note submitted to the Viceroy, he referred to the dominance of the 'young Party' Muslims, led by Mohamed Ali :

> A few moderates may grumble here and there, and a few conservative Mohomedans may argue that the League does not represent their community. But they *do* nothing. They are voiceless in public; they do not hold meetings; they have completely lost command of the Press. For all practical purposes they have, for the time at least, disappeared as a separate party.[3]

In recent years, some historians have seen in Mohamed Ali a charmer and nothing more; a politician greedy for power, an

1 Sydenham to Hardinge, 18 March 1913, Hardinge Papers (86), CUL.

2 Meston to Chelmsford, 20 August 1917, Meston Papers, MSS. EUR. F. 136(1), IOL.

3 Note by Meston, 7 February 1917, *ibid* (17).

irresponsible declaimer who drove himself and his followers from one disaster to another.[4] According to Francis Robinson, Mohamed Ali belonged to a group of 'Young Party' Muslims who manufactured issues and whipped up agitations to keep their newspapers going, their organisations active and their coffers full.[5] 'The Kanpur Mosque Fund, the Khilafat Fund, the Angora Fund, the names trace the path trodden by India's political gold diggers', concludes Robinson.[6]

In sharp contrast to Robinson's unsympathetic assessment are studies which tend to glorify the role of Mohamed Ali by emphasising his unflinching commitment to the tenets of Islam and his selfless devotion to the causes of its followers.[7] In Pakistan he is regarded as one of the exponents of the two-nation theory and an architect of the new nation. This is reflected in the following observation :

> In the face of his unshakeable faith in Islamic ideology and his advocacy of the right of self-determination for the people of northern areas—Muslim majority provinces—it would be unfair on the part of a historian not to include him in the list of prominent leaders who contributed in their own way to the march of the Muslim nation on the way to its final destination.[8]

In India, on the other hand, ingenious apologists and admirers

4 This, in essence, is the argument of M. Mujeeb. See *The Indian Muslims*, (London, 1967). Two extremely perceptive essays in Urdu offer a critical appreciation of Mohamed Ali's role. See, Abdul Huq, *Chand Hum A'sr* (Karachi, 1952 edn.); I. Askari, 'Mohamed Ali: Ek Sada-i-Shikast Sa'az', *Aligarh Magazine*, 1960-61.

5 Robinson, *Separatism Among Indian Muslims: The Politics of the United Provinces' Muslims, 1860-1923* (Cambridge, 1974), pp. 178-9. The interpretation of Robinson is generally followed by Judith M. Brown in her earlier published work: *Gandhi's Rise to Power: Indian Politics 1915-1922*, (Cambridge, 1971).

6 *Ibid.*, p. 354.

7 Such an analysis is offered by Abdul Majid Daryabadi, Afzal Iqbal, Rais Ahmad Jafri, and Ishtiaq Husain Qureshi. Their works have been referred to throughout this study.

8 Moinul Haq (ed.), *Mohamed Ali: Life and Work* (Karachi, 1978), p. 41. The essays included in various 'Special Numbers', published in Pakistan, have highlighted Mohamed Ali's contribution to the making of Pakistan, e.g., *Nigar*, Nov.—Dec., 1976; *Maulana Mohamed Ali Jauhar Sadi Conference*, Karachi, 1978.

extol Mohamed Ali's contribution to the cause of Hindu-Muslim amity, his identification with the struggle for freedom, and the fact that he waged a continuing smouldering war against all forms of authority that demanded unquestioning faith. According to such accounts, Mohamed Ali's presidential address at the Kakinada Congress in December 1923 and the speech at the plenary session of the Round Table Conference in November 1930 bear eloquent testimony to his nationalist concerns.[9] This impression of a nationalist *par excellence* has been sedulously cultivated to project the Maulana both as the leading light in the camp of nationalist Muslims and as a consistent and fearless adherent to the Congress movement.[10] It is also aimed at countering the notion that, soon after the All-Parties Conference at Delhi in 1924, he drifted from the side of the Congress and parted company with his chief, Gandhi, to that of communalism.

Such assessments need to be reexamined in the light of fresh materials that have recently been made available. In so doing, the aim is neither to belittle Mohamed Ali's participation in the national movement nor to deny his sacrifices. There can be no doubt that he played a key role in heightening Muslim political consciousness and in organising the massive Khilafat protest. But after the collapse of the Khilafat and Non-cooperation movements, Mohamed Ali was cast in a different mould. He not only identified himself with seemingly communal causes, but also led the crusade against the Nehru Report. While his admirers and detractors have continued to produce a steady stream of literature about his pan-Islamic proclivities, they have not adequately investigated the later phase of his political activities.

Any fresh analysis of Mohamed Ali cannot evade his diverse concerns, his fluctuating loyalties, and the contradictions in his politics. This essay is focussed on these aspects. At the same time, it seeks to enlarge our understanding of Mohamed Ali's role in and his contribution to Indian politics during the anti-colonial movement. An attempt is also made to explore the circumstances

9 Moin Shakir, *Khilafat to Partition* (Delhi, 1972), pp. 70, 74, 86; S.M. Hadi, *Ali Biradaran awr unka zamana* (Delhi, 1978).

10 Shan Muhammad, *Freedom Movement in India—The role of Ali Brothers* (Delhi, 1978); *A'aj Kal*, Publications Division, 1978; *Jamia* (Delhi), 'Mohamed Ali Number', April 1979, Jan-Feb., 1980.

which facilitated his emergence from obscurity to a dramatic assertion of power during the Khilafat and Non-cooperation campaigns.

This is not, however, a conventional biography. Nor is this a detailed survey of Muslim politics between 1911 and 1930, an aspect which has been adequately discussed by several historians of modern India. Our purpose is to enlarge our knowledge of Mohamed Ali, a manifestly central figure in the political changes of those years and a representative of a new genre of politics which was to become the hallmark of Muslim concerns in the early decades of this century.

From the non-official sources and the records of government departments, it is possible to plot the main landmarks of Mohamed Ali's political life. These include the private papers of British officials and of Indian leaders connected with the national movement. Mohamed Ali's own writings are quite considerable. As a journalist he was called upon to write hundreds of routine letters; as one of the key organisers of the Khilafat movement he wrote hundreds more; in the course his mission to Europe[11] and his internment he wrote enough letters to fill a large volume. The main topic covered in these is politics, but the tone constantly varies from boredom and depression, on the one hand, to exhiliration and conviction on the other, now relaxed and desultory. now indulging in flights of fantasy or burlesque. A flair for the dramatic, coupled with a wry self-awareness; a temperament that allowed the fullest reins to intellectual enthusiasms while never fully realizing personal ones. This complexity, not rare but fascinating in Mohamed Ali's case, can be discerned in his correspondence and speeches.

Besides an autobiographical account—*My Life: A Fragment*—Mohamed Ali wrote a number of pamphlets and hundreds of articles for the *Comrade* and *Hamdard.* He also wrote enough poems to fill a not-so-slim volume[12], and miscellaneous historical

11 Some of his correspondence from Europe has been compiled by *Muhammad Sarwar* in *Maulana Mohamed Ali Ke Europe Ke Safar* (Lahore, 1941). In general, however, his correspondence and speeches have not been systematically compiled. The few collections published are either incomplete or indifferently edited. For example, *Nuqqush* (Lahore), 'Makatib Number', November 1957, vol. I; S. Muhammad (ed.), *Unpublished letters of the Ali Brothers* (Delhi, 1979); Abu Salman Shahjahanpuri (ed.), *Siyasi Maktubat Rais ul-Ahrar* (Karachi, 1978); Abadi Bano and Ghate (eds.), *Mr. Shaukat Ali and Mr. Mohamed Ali: Collection* (Delhi, 1918).

12 A. Rauf (ed.), *Mohamed Ali awr unki Shairi* (Karachi, 1963); Nur-ur Rahman (ed.), *Divan-i-Jauhar* (Karachi, 1962).

literary and political pieces enough to fill another.[13] Such rich and varied materials illuminate various facets of Mohamed Ali's personality.

13 Some of his articles have been included in R.A. Jafri (ed.), *Selections from Mohamed Ali's Comrade* (Lahore, 1965); M. Sarwar (ed.), *Mazameen-i-Mohamed Ali*, 2 vols., (Delhi, 1938); R.A. Jafri (ed.), *Ifadat-i-Mohamed Ali* (Hyderabad. n.d.).

1

THE FORMATIVE YEARS

Mohamed Ali was born on 10 December 1878 in a prosperous but not so distinguished family of Rampur.[1] His grandfather, Sheikh Ali Baksh (1813-1867), was a petty official in the Court of Nawab Mohammad Yusuf Khan. But his fortunes improved during the 1857 revolt when he actively helped the British in quelling the disturbances at Bareilly and Moradabad. In 1859, he received a *Khilat* and a rent free or a *muafi* land with an annual income of Rs. 13,000.[2] Even after his death in 1867, Ali Baksh's family continued to reap the rewards of loyalty to the Raj. Abdul Ali (1848-1880), the father of the Ali Brothers, enjoyed the patronage of the Nawab of Rampur and was one of his favourite courtiers. But he died young, leaving his young widow, Abadi Bano Begum (1852-1924), the responsibility of bringing up the children.[3] This was no easy task, for Abdul Ali had incurred heavy debts because of his extravagance.[4] The Begum's own family lost out during the Mutiny for its involvement in the *jehad* against the British; the property of Maulvis Basharat Ali, Vilayat Ali Khan and Meherban Ali Khan-acquired through the generosity of the Mughal Emperors-

1 For biographical information, see Afzal Iqbal, *Life and Times of Mohamed Ali* (Delhi, 1978 edn.); R.A. Jafri, *Sirat-i-Mohamed Ali* (Delhi, 1932).

2 Mohammad Ayub Qadiri, 'Maulana Mohamed Ali Ka Khandaan', in A.S. Shahjahanpuri (ed), *Maulana Mohamed Ali: Sawanah wa Khidma'at*, Journal of Government National College, Karachi.

3 Abadi Bano was in direct line of succession of a number of Ministers of the Mughals, the last of whom was Nawab Shamsuddin Khan who retired from his office into the privacy of his home at Amroha.

4 *Comrade*, 21 November 1924.

was confiscated by the British.[5] Mohamed Ali had thus inherited the mixed legacy of collaboration and opposition to the Raj. He was to continue this legacy during his eventful public life.

Undeterred by the limited resources of her family and the heavy debt incurred by a spend-thrift husband, Abadi Bano sent her children to the Bareilly High School. The moment she was approached by Azimuddin Khan (General of Rampur forces), wrote Mohamed Ali, 'she consented to send Zulfiqar bhai to Bareilly, and people wondered that any mother should be so lacking in love for her children as to send them away from home while they are still so young'.[6] This was a remarkably bold, though unpopular, decision because of widespread Muslim prejudice that prevailed against western education. The story of Syed Ahmad Khan's trials and tribulations in founding the Aligarh College and the hostile response to his efforts are well known. Equally known are those leading families which generously supported the efforts of Syed Ahmad Khan and insisted on sending their scions to the college at Aligarh-'the well known, and in a way notorious, institution founded on the model of English Public School'. The frail figure of Abadi Bano belonged to one such family. All her children-Zulfiqar, Shaukat, Mohamed-joined the Aligarh College in search for a safe and secure future.

In the graph of Mohamed Ali's life, the steep arc of youth is missing; we see only the flattened curve of maturity. For instance, little is known about his early life, except that he read a few Persian classics, learned to read-without understanding-the Quran in Arabic, and absorbed the routine of the religious rituals practised in his Sunni home. His activities in Aligarh (1890-98) are also not known, for his contemporaries-Sajjad Hyder Yaldaram, Mohammad Yaqub, T.A.K. Sherwani, Syed Raza Ali, Khaliquz-zaman, and Zafar Ali Khan-have left few impressions of their future political mentor. But the few stray references reveal that Mohamed Ali left no indelible impression on his teachers and fellow students. He was a keen organiser of *mushairas*, an infrequent contributor to the college magazine, and a some what indifferent

5 Ayub Qadiri, *op. cit*; David Lelyveld, 'Three Aligarh Students: Aftab Ahmad Khan, Ziauddin Ahmad and Mohammad Ali'. *Modern Asian Studies*, VIII (1954).

6 *Comrade*, 5 December 1924.

cricketer.[7] He shared his brother's love for the 'noble and manly game of cricket', but seemed less confident in the twenty-two yard strip. He played cricket because it was fashionable to do so in the precincts of the Aligarh College.[8]

The Aligarh College of Mohamed Ali's days, modelled after Oxford and Cambridge, followed an ardent and sustained pro-British policy; in the words of its Principal, Theodore Beck, it produced 'some very nice and well bred youngmen'. A feudal spirit reigned over it and the goal of an average student was government service.[9] It was hard to be otherwise. Syed Ahmad Khan, the genius behind the founding of the College, considered education as the sole means for the regeneration of the Muslim community and regarded Anglo-Muslim rapprochement as a necessary condition for the improvement of its position in Indian society. 'The well-being of the people of India and especially of the Musalmans', he wrote, 'lies in leading a quiet life under the benign rule of the English government'.[10] The College of his dream occupied a pivotal position in the life of the Muslim community because of its role in making Muslims 'worthy and useful subjects of the British Crown',[11] in grooming students to go on to British Universities, and in training them for government employment. This was the *raison d'etre* of the M.A.O. College.

Syed Ahmad's expectations were fulfilled during his lifetime. The College, organised and dominated by Beck and his lieutenants, successfully fostered the spirit of 'manly games and manly sentiments'. Students cultivated English habits and tastes, expressed loyalty to the crown by decorating their rooms with potraits of

7 Some of these impressions are recorded in Jafri, *Sirat-i-Mohamed Ali*, pp. 12-13.

8 Syed Raza Ali, who joined the Aligarh College in 1898, recalled the emphasis on games and the popularity of those who excelled in sports. *A'am'al Nama*, pp. 75-6.

9 Jawaharlal Nehru noted in his *Autobiography*: 'Aligarh College did fine work, produced a large number of competent men, and changed the whole tone of the Muslim intelligentsia, but still could not wholly get out of the framework in which it was built—a feudal spirit reigned over it, and the goal of the average student's ambition was government service. *An Autobiography* (London, 1936), p. 464.

10 *Aligarh Institute Gazette*, 3 April 1894.

11 M.S. Jain, *The Aligarh Movement: Its Origin and Development, 1858-1906* (Agra, 1965), pp. 53-4.

Queen Victoria and the Prince of Wales, and paid heed to repeated admonitions to avoid political discussions. The so-called political debates at the Siddons Union Club, organised for the development of elocution and debating talents, were a tame affair.

The arguments against the Congress movement, so vigorously voiced by Syed Ahmad Khan and so systematically formulated by Beck, also evoked a favourable response in Aligarh. On 18 January 1888, the Siddons Union Club expressed its disapproval of the Congress methods and barred all pro-Congress newspapers.[12] The political ideology of the College, particularly in relation to the British, was best summed up in the following written rules of the Union Club :

> No matter shall be discussed which raises the question of the permanence of British Rule, nor any subject which involves the necessity of the speakers...taking up a disloyal or seditious attitude towards the British Government in its internal policy or relations...[13]

Mohamed Ali seemed comfortable in the isolated and intense environment of the College. He was also on the best of terms with the authorities, including Beck,[14] cultivating Theodore Morison after his return from England and, in 1904, supporting the Principal's decision to suspend Hasrat Mohani, Secretary of the *Anjuman-i-Moalla*, for organising a *mushaira* where 'obseene' poetry was recited.[15] His favourite pastimes were cricket and *mushairas* with the scholar, Shibli Nomani, providing the occasional intellectual stimuli.[16] He shared, along with other students of his

12 D. Lelyveld, *Aligarh's First Generation: Muslim Solidarity in British India* (Princeton University Press, 1978), p. 318; S.K. Bhatnagar, *History of the M.A.O. College Aligarh* (Aligarh, 1969), p. 87.

13 Lelyveld, *op. cit.*, p. 319.

14 Iqbal, *Life and Times*, p. 25.

15 Majnu Gorakhpuri, 'Hasrat Mohani', *Urdu Adab* (Hasrat Number), 1952, p. 80. I owe this reference to Mr. Atiq Siddiqi.

16 According to Mohamed Ali's own testimony: 'Aligarh itself presented one bright spot in all this cimmerian darkness and I must not omit to mention it. This was no other than a College Professor of rare whom Sir Syed Ahmad Khan had been able to attach to Aligarh. He was Shibli Numani, Professor of Arabic and Persian, an ardent lover of poetry and of Islamic History. . . . His ordinary daily lectures at Aligarh on Persian and Arabic

background, the limited ambition of securing 'a nomination for the post of Subordinate Magistrate or Land Revenue Collector'.[17] But the 'Big Brother', impressed with Mohamed Ali's 'unexpected success' at the B.A. examinations, had other plans. He raised money to send the younger brother to England. In Mohamed Ali's own words:

> . . . My brother had now far higher aspirations for me, and I have not yet met his equal in planning greatly and, what is more, also executing greatly . . . The raising of funds . . . was nothing short of a miracle, and unlike most miracles in this unbelieving age, he certainly managed to come off. So, before the proverbial nine days of wonder were over, I was on the high seas in the Indian Ocean in the teeth of a raging monsoon, bound for England . . . [18]

Mohamed Ali reached London in September 1898 and, within weeks of his arrival, found his way into English middle class society with the help of the family of T.W. Arnold and Theodore Beck. Fazl-i-Husain, who arrived in England about the same time, described Mohamed Ali 'as a jolly good fellow, very quick in making friends'.[19] Together they spent 'exceedingly pleasant evenings', discussing literary, philosophical and political issues.[20]

On 11 October 1898, Mohamed Ali reached Oxford to join Lincoln College to study Modern History. He matriculated a year later and secured a second in 1902, 'missing a first, as I learnt subsequently from my tutor, by a very narrow margin'.[21] His tutors were not only impressed with his extraordinary vigour, commonsense, resourcefulness but also considered him 'well fitted for

were most attractive, but unfortunately for me, he had retired from the College before I matriculated from the school attached to it, and so I could not attend them. Nevertheless, I was fortunate enough, although still a school boy, to attend his all too brief lectures to the undergraduates on the Quran'.

A. Iqbal (ed.), *My Life a Fragment: An Autobiographical Sketch of Maulana Mohamed Ali* (Lahore, 1974, edn.), p. 23.

17 *Ibid.*, p. 28.

18 *Ibid.*

19 Azim Husain, *Fazl-i-Husain: A Political Biography* (Bombay, 1936), p. 20.

20 *Ibid.*, p. 20. Also, Iqbal, *Life and Times*, pp. 31-32.

21 Mohamed Ali to Dewan Tek Chand, n.d., Mohamed Ali Papers, JMI.

doing good work in an educational post in India which is the career he desires'.[22] James Williams, Fellow and Law Lecturer of Lincoln College, instructed Mohamed Ali in Roman and English Law and noticed his

> great capacity for acquiring and remembering information and in addition has a considerable sense of style. He is very industrious and has made great progress since his admission to this college. It appears to me that he has just the qualifications necessary for a position in the educational service of India.[23]

Such sweet words could hardly provide consolation to Mohamed Ali after his failure at the civil service examination, 'thanks to an English spring and a youngman's more or less foolish fancy'. Mohamed Ali was bitter and disappointed. So was Shaukat Ali. A degree in Modern History was hardly the reward for his investment. But he swallowed the bitter pill and welcomed the return of his brother in 1902.

Success eluded Mohamed Ali after his return to India. His desire to teach at the Aligarh College was thwarted by Theodore Morison and, according to some accounts, by Mohsinul Mulk; so he sought refuge in his home town where he joined the Education Department.[24] But his restless soul found no peace. In November 1902, he threatened to resign because his endeavour to initiate reforms in the Education Department was effectively countered by jealous, intriguing and old-fashioned officials.[25] But friends prevented him from adopting such a reckless course and cautioned him against pressing reforms. A friend from Bournemoth, who had served in several princely states in India, wrote on 1 December 1912:

> I hope you have not been precipitate in throwing up employment at Rampur......I can quite understand what you write as to the

22 Testimonial of Rector, Lincoln College, 19 October 1901, *ibid*; W. Warde Fowler was impressed with his paper on Macbeth 'which not having been written by anyone but a man of ability, capable of thinking for himself'.

23 Testimonial of James Williams, 14 October 1901, *ibid*.

24 *My Life: A Fragment*, p. 30.

25 Mohamed Ali to Mahfuz Ali, 14 January 1919 (in Urdu), Muhammad Sarwar (ed.), *Khutut-i-Mohamed Ali* (Delhi, 1940), pp. 252-54.

> constant petty intrigue that goes on, and can sympathise with your outraged feelings in this matter. Your education and experience of English life have opened your eyes to much that you did not see before, and have unsettled you and made you discontented. *But you must not go back to bayonets.* Reform out at the point of that weapon would not be worth much. Time, patience, experience and forbearance are, I think, what we must rely on. It is a mistake to try to force things (and)to compress the work of centuries into a pint bottle. I always felt that we were too much in a hurry too—to thrust our western ideas down eastern throats. After all is said there is much that is beautiful and dignified in the old eastern life and manners......I want to persuade you not to be too impetuous. As you grow older you will learn patience, and see things more in their proportion.[26]

All such advice was in vain. Mohamed Ali resigned in 1902 and took up a responsible but subordinate post in far-off Baroda in the Opium Department—the sort of post conventionally filled by men of his background.

The princely state of Baroda seemed to offer a bright prospect because its ruler, Gaekwad Sayaji Rao (1875-1936), was favourably disposed towards Mohamed Ali and was receptive to his ideas on revenue administration. The Gaekwad regarded him as some one on whose shoulders he could place the burden of administrative work—the man who got papers drawn up, orders sent out, correspondence carried on, and records kept. But jealous officials, resenting Mohamed Ali's enthusiasm for reforms and his proximity to the Gaekwad, made life wholly unpleasant. Though he kept himself in the public eye by articles in the press and speeches at Conferences, Mohamed Ali was desperate to leave for Bhopal by the end of 1906.[27] Dunlop Smith, a friend and well-wisher, urged

26 1 December 1911, MAP.

27 This is evident from Mohamed Ali's correspondence with Syed Mahfuz Ali. It is, however, clear that Mohamed Ali took a keen interest in developments around. Although exaggerated claims are made about his profound influence on the deliberations of the Muslim League in December 1906, he was nevertheless regarded as a potentially bright recruit. In February 1907, he delivered two lectures in Allahabad which seem to have attracted some notice. A month later, he prepared a complete text of the proceedings of the Muslim League meeting which was published as "Green Book No. 1". This may have prompted an explanation from an official.

him to stay. 'I quite understand that your surroundings are not always congenial', he wrote, 'but after all whose are in every respect'.[28] Around this time, the *Thoughts on the Present Discontent*, based on articles published in the *Times of India* and the *Indian Spectator*, was released. Mohamed Ali sent a copy to the Viceroy with the hope

> that this little booklet in which a conscientious effort is made to express without malice but with a candour born of confidence in my own honesty of purpose and in its just appreciation by others the true state of the feelings of His Majesty's subjects in India would meet with the sympathy and encouragement which India has learnt to associate now with the name of Edward the Peace-Maker just as she had so long associated it with the name of our late lamented sovereign Lady Victoria.[26]

The Viceroy was pleased, expressing his 'hearty agreement with much that you put forward' and wishing 'the book the wide circulation it deserves'.[30]

Mohamed Ali was destined to remain in Baroda until 1910, but his heart was never at rest.[31] Activity and companionship were the drugs he craved. He yearned for the *mushairas*, which was his passion from the college days, and the *mehfils* where he could transmit the flame of his intellectual excitement to others. The drab and routine work at the Opium Department, combined with the unfamiliar cultural mileu and the hostility of his colleagues, could offer no solace to the bouyant and exuberant Mohamed Ali. 'In spite of being an Indian and having received a very similar education to the rest of the Baroda officials', he complained to the Gaekwad of Baroda, 'I found that I differ from them in almost

'I sent in a reply', wrote Mohamed Ali, before the Council. In response, a general confidential circular was issued to government servants. They were told not to contribute articles which were likely to create communal animosity'. Mohamed Ali to Mahfuz Ali, 14 January 1910, *Khutut*, pp. 252-54. For a summary of Mohamed Ali's two speeches delivered in Allahabad, see Home Poll. B, 149, 1913, NAI.

28 Dunlop Smith to Mohamed Ali, 31 January 1907, MAP.

29 Mohamed Ali to Dunlop Smith, 5 December 1907, *ibid.*

30 Mohamed Ali to G.K. Gokhale, 8 February 1908, Gokhale Papers (341), National Archives of India (NAI).

31 Mohamed Ali to Mahfuz Ali, 14 January 1910, *Khutut*, pp. 252-4.

everything, and that it was difficult if not impossible for me to be received by them as one of their own number'.[32]

For the time being the prospect of a government job—Assistant Private Secretary to the Governor of Bombay and Assistant Directorship of Criminal Intelligence—seemed to be the only silver lining in an otherwise dismal picture. 'Sir Dunlop Smith and Sir Harold Stuart are trying their best to secure an appointment for me, and I hope their effort will bear fruit', wrote Mohamed Ali to his school friend, Syed Mahfuz Ali, in January 1910.[33] But hopes were soon turned into despair when he was bluntly told that 'the expenses of an Indian Private Secretary would (not) be justified at present', and that his 'lack of experience of detective work was a bar for a post in Home Department'.[34] 'I am sorry to give you such a depressing reply', wrote H.A. Stuart, 'but I keep you in mind and if anything turns up you may rest assured that I shall not forget you'.[35] Clearly, senior officials enjoyed Mohamed Ali's company and admired his talents, but were chary of pushing him forward for government employment. The only exception was Michael O'Dwyer, later Governor of the Punjab, who recommended him to the ruler of Jaora State. But Mohamed Ali flatly refused the offer. This petty state could hardly assuage his thirst for participation in great events, even in a subordinate capacity.

Repeated failures left Mohamed Ali with one option—a career of journalism. 'The affairs of my community', he wrote, 'made it the only avenue through which I could hope to reach a place in which I could prove of any appreciable use to it, while still earning a livelihood'.[36] Indeed Mohamed Ali's journalistic venture met with immediate success and he achieved uprecedented prominence during the tumultuous decade following the revocation of Bengal's partition. As a journalist he did not quite make the first-grade, but his forthright and unmistakable style is as fresh as when it was written. The *Comrade*, launched on 14 January 1911, became the main spokesman of the angry and restless Muslim intelligentsia and its energetic editor was able to carve out his own independent

32 Mohamed Ali to the Gaekwad of Baroda, n.d., MAP.
33 *Khutut*, pp. 252-4.
34 G.S. Clark to Mohamed Ali, 2 November 1909; also, Dunlop Smith to Mohamed Ali, 30 October 1909, MAP.
35 H.A. Stuart to Mohamed Ali, 10 December 1909, *ibid*
36 *My Life: A Fragment*, p. 32.

sphere of influence in the United Provinces, the nerve-centre of Muslim intellectual, religious and political life.[37] 'No paper has so much influence with the students as the *Comrade*, and no individual has the authority over them which is exercised by Mohamed Ali', reported the U.P. government in 1914.[38] When, at the beginning of his internment, Mohamed Ali wanted to stop the *Hamdard*, Vilayat Ali wrote begging him not to do so: 'I don't approve of your decision and I don't think many will. . .You can't imagine what the loss of Hamdard will mean to us—the Musalmans'.[39] There were other newspapers as well : the *Al-Hilal* (Calcutta), the *Muslim Gazette* (Lucknow), the *Al Bashir* (Etawah), the *Zul Qarnain* (Budaun), and the *Zamindar* (Lahore). But the influence of the *Comrade* and the *Hamdard* was unrivalled. They performed the important role of providing a framework for the uneasiness and dissatisfaction of the Muslim educated elite, moulded their attitudes towards government and towards other groups in the community and, above all, focussed on religious issues which concerned many Muslims. The *Comrade* of the early years testifies to its vigorous and passionate interest in the Turkish cause, especially the retention of the Turks of their first capital, Adrianople. The same newspaper splashed the Kanpur mosque incident across its columns, revelling in every detail from the screams of the dying to the blood-bespattered pavement.[40] The Viceroy sensed trouble and provided the healing touch. Mohamed Ali and his colleagues were mollified.[41] 'Kanpur in the end', he wrote to Hardinge, 'became the battle ground of Muslim self-realization and civilian self-aggrandizement, and I desire to detract nothing from your sagacity in trying to effect a compromise in saying that the result of the struggle was a victory for the Muslim solidarity'.[42]

37 For the influence of *Comrade*, see K.M. Ashraf, 'Aligarh ki Siyasi Zindagi', *Aligarh Magazine* (Special Number: Aligarh Number) 1953-1955, p. 164. 'Throughout the country, there was only one voice which was heard by the people of the north and the south, the east and the west, by the educated and the illiterate, the *ulama* and the ignorant. . . .' Abdul Majid Daryabadi, *Maqalat-i-Majid* (Bombay, n.d.), p. 233-34.

38 Home Poll. D., December 1914, 31, NAI.

39 Vilayat Ali to Mohamed Ali, 20 August 1915, MAP.

40 Robinson, *op. cit.*, pp. 202, 213.

41 Hardinge to Butler, 31 July 1913; Hardinge to Zulfiqar Ali Khan, Chief Minister, Patiala State, Hardinge Papers, Microfilm, NML.

42 Mohamed Ali to Hardinge, 24 April 1919, MAP.

In pursuance of his goals, Mohamed Ali chose the precincts of the Aligarh College to conduct his various agitational campaigns. He had a unique opportunity to do so. The College, known for many years as the most 'benighted' and conservative of the institutions, suddenly exploded into political activity after the death of its founder. The agitation against the Nagri resolution of 18 April 1900, organised by Mohsinul Mulk and other tall poppies of the College, confronted the British with the most serious Muslim movement of dissidence which they had faced in India since the Mutiny. It represented a trend to steer the Muslim community on a course different from that plotted by Syed Ahmad Khan.[43] Disillusioned with the politics of collaboration and increasingly unhappy with the British staff which 'wished to rule over the students in the same fashion in which the collectors play the autocratic despots in their small empires of districts',[44] Aligarh students also threw to the winds all the caution that they had learnt at the feet of Syed Ahmad Khan. In 1905 a shocked Archbold, Principal of the College, witnessed the Students Union vote overwhelmingly in favour of the Swadeshi movement in Bengal.[45] This was followed by a strike in February 1907, caused by the expulsion of three prominent student leaders : Raja Ghulam Husain, T.A.K. Sherwani and Abdur Rahman Bijnori. The strike, sparked off by a minor incident at the Exhibition Grounds, was the culmination of long-standing grievances against the British staff, and was viewed as a 'spontaneous spirit of self-assertion on the part of those placed under control'.[46]

Both the Urdu agitation and the students' strike represented extremely new trends in Aligarh politics. Contemporaries never tired of pointing out how, just a few years before they appeared,

43 For details of the agitation, see Robinson, *op. cit.*, pp. 135-37; Mushirul Hasan, *Nationalism and Communal Politics in India, 1916-1928* (Delhi, 1979), pp. 48-50.

44 *Mahratta*, 3 March 1907.

45 *Indian People*, 10 December 1905, Report on Native Newspapers, (United Provinces), 1905, p. 402. On the motion: 'The Muslims if they desire to be a prominent people in India, should join in efforts for national advancement', introduced in the Student's Union, ninety voted for and only six voted against. *Tribune*, 9 May 1906.

46 Letter to the Editor, *Tribune*, 29 March 1907. For a lesser known account of the strike, see Mohammad Amin Zuberi, *Hayat-i-Muhsin* (Aligarh, 1934), pp. 136-140.

there was not the slightest sign of their imminence. This earlier quiesence was attributed to the influence of Syed Ahmad Khan, and to the predominance of conservative landed interests in the Board of Trustees.

During the first decade of the twentieth century, however, politics at Aligarh was gradually being radicalised partly in consequence of the growing Congress movement, but largely in reaction to British administrative and bureaucratic policies. This trend was most clearly discernible in the agitation against Anthony Macdonnel's Nagri resolution and in the students' strike.[47] Its dangerous potential was recognised by Mohsinul Mulk who warned Archbold that Muslims 'already feel a little disappointed, and young Muslims seem to have a sympathy for the "Congress" '.[48] This was confirmed by, among others, W.S. Marris, the Collector of Aligarh. He noticed the radical strain in Aligarh politics, and, in 1907, wrote:

> How far the Aligarh movement has taken on a political colour is plain to any onlooker. The prominence of Aftab Ahmad Khan among the trustees, and of demagogues like Muhammad Ali and Shaukat Ali; the inception of the university movement as a counterblast to the Hindu University scheme; the enlisting of all national leaders like the Aga Khan; its association with the All-India Muslim League and All-India Muslim Educational Conference—these are all symptoms of one policy. Aligarh is destined to be the focus of all Muhammadan intelligence and activity in India. Begun as a defensive move, it is already acquiring an offensive character. . . .It has already lost its reliance on Englishmen and its trust in English methods and ideals. The danger I forsee is that if it is indulged and uncontrolled it will develop rapidly on decidedly anti-English lines.[49]

The prophecy of Marris came true during the Turko-Italian War, the Muslim University movement, and the Kanpur mosque incident

47 See, Hasan, *Nationalism and Communal Politics*, pp. 48-51.

48 Quoted in R. Wasti, *Lord Minto and the Indian Nationalist Movement, 1905-1910* (Oxford, 1964), p. 63.

49 Quoted in I.A. Gilbert, 'Autonomy and Consensus under the Raj', in S.H. Rudolph and L.I. Rudolph (eds.), *Education and Politics in India* (Delhi, 1972), pp. 198-99.

when the College, under the leadership of some of its products like Hasrat Mohani, Zafar Ali Khan and Raja Ghulam Husain, became the focus of agitational politics. Their doyen was Mohamed Ali. Along with Shaukat Ali, the younger brother maintained his overriding concern in Aligarh affairs. Shaukat, who took extended leave from the Opium Department to join the Aga Khan in the fund-raising campaign for the Muslim University, was Honorary Secretary of the Old Boys' Association (in 1912-1915) and one of the joint-secretaries of the proposed Muslim University Committee. When he was forced to resign in 1915, Mohamed Ali was elected as a Trustee of the College by the Old Boys' Association. But this was small reward for the ambitious Mohamed Ali who was anxious to use the University, and the movement to create it, as vehicles for popular mobilization.[50] The University, he declared in his maiden speech in October 1904, provided the glittering vision of pan-Islamism—a common centre where Muslims from all parts of the world would congregate and make active again a common Islamic consciousness that will be powerful in upholding Muslim interests in India and elsewhere.[51] This speech, modelled on the style of Edmund Burke and with quotations from Latin, Arabic, Persian, Urdu and English literature, proved the swan song of the first phase of the Muslim University movement.[52]

In 1907, Mohamed Ali supported—some said fomented—a major student strike that resulted in the resignation of Mohsinul Mulk as

50 Gail Minault and David Lelyveld have argued that the University movement harboured within it many conflicts, both conceptual and personal. Its supporters included professional educators concerned with the quality of the university, as well as professional politicians anxious to use the university, and the movement to create it as vehicles for popular mobilization. See 'The Campaign for a Muslim University', *Modern Asian Studies*, vol. 8, 1974, p. 145.

51 *Comrade*, 28 January 1911; Such a vision was shared by Mohamed Ali's contemporaries. Notice the observation of Syed Abdul Qadir: 'Oh! how we look with anxious eyes, to the future, when a Muslim University will be launched into existence—a university that will. . . encourage true culture and will be the nursery of true Muslims. 'The Proposed Mohammadan University', *The Muslim Review* (Allahabad), October 1910, p. 288. Also, M.T. Kaderbhoy, 'The Muslim University', *The Muslim Review*, July-August 1911, p. 501.

52 Gail Minault & David Lelyveld, 'The Campaign For a Muslim University', *Modern Asian Studies*, p. 157.

Hony. Secretary and his replacement with Viqarul Mulk.[53] His critique of the College administration, published in the Lahore *Observer*, and his factional disputes with Aftab Ahmad Khan's 'ruling clique' made him the *bete noire* of both the English staff and the Board of Trustees. The English staff of the College complained to E.M. Forster that they were neither 'trusted to give the help they had hoped nor could they make some way with the students—not much, owing to the influence of the *Comrade*, a forward Islamic newspaper'. The Muslims, they noted, 'had an air of desperation, which may be habitual, but was impressive'.[54]

During the Turko-Italian War, Mohamed Ali maintained his close links with the College, encouraging dissent against the British-dominated administration, holding 'secret' meetings, and lecturing upon the evils falling upon Islam in Tripoli, Morocco, Persia and Turkey. 'The College is becoming a hot-bed of sedition', wrote an alarmed Viceroy and wondered if anything could be done to prevent students 'being tampered with'. He went on to add : 'I regard Mohamed Ali as a dangerous malcontent who must always be reckoned with as an element of strife'.[55]

53 Mohamed Ali to Gokhale, 8 February 1908, Gokhale Papers (341).

54 Quoted in P.N. Furbank, *E.M. Forster: A Life: The Growth of the Novelist, 1879-1914* (London, 1978), p. 227.

55 Hardinge to Meston, 14 November 1912, Hardinge to Butler, 29 October 1912, Butler to Hardinge, 3 November 1912, Hardinge Papers, Microfilm, NML. Malcolm Hailey, Chief Commissioner of Delhi, described him as 'the centre and inspiration of the Pan-Islamic movement.' W.M. Hailey to H.H. Wheeler, 1 May 1915, Home Poll. D, May 1915, 36, NAI.

2

ASCENT TO LEADERSHIP

From 1900 onwards, the government introduced a series of administrative and bureaucratic reforms in order to pacify the Hindu revivalists in U.P. and the anti-partition enthusiasts in Bengal.[1] Some of these reforms caused great uneasiness amongst Muslims, threatened the Anglo-Muslim *entente cordiale* in India, provided a powerful stimulus for the growth of political radicalism, and paved the way for the emergence of a pro-Congress group, particularaly in Bengal and U.P. where government policies disturbed the *status quo* most.[2] The group, identified by government officials as the 'hot-headed Nationalist Party', stood for agitational politics as opposed to the politics of subservience advocated by Syed Ahmad Khan, had no faith in the beneficence of British rule, and emphasised the importance of claiming concessions through agitation and vigorous protest. It saw that the Swadeshi movement against the partition of Bengal had achieved results: compared to this their traditional loyalty seemed unrewarding. 'Agitate and you will get what you want; remain calm and you will have your heads chopped off. This is the moral we are given', observed a Muslim correspondent from Calcutta.[3] The anti-Muslim bias of Anthony Macdonnell's policies in U.P., the reunification of Bengal in 1911, the rejection of the Muslim University scheme in 1912, and the Kanpur mosque incident in 1913 seemed to demonstrate

1 The impact of some of these reforms have been carefully analysed by Robinson in his chapter: 'Threats to the Urdu-speaking elite in the late nineteenth century'.

2 Hasan, *Nationalism and Communal Politics*, pp. 44-64.

3 *Mussalman*, 12 January, 1912.

the validity of the view that radical self-help was a better solution than mendicancy.

The radical strain in Muslim politics also had a profound impact on Muslim leadership and its attitude towards the Congress. The old school of aristocratic Muslim politicians stood discredited because their policy of collaboration had proved a failure, and the 'younger men' — the men of *Nai Raushni* and the representatives of 'new ideals' and 'new force' — seized the initiative.[4] They neither felt the constraining hand of the moderates in the Muslim League nor were they committed to constitutional politics. They realized, however, the pressing need to reorganise their organisation which would speak for and defend the community's interests. This view was articulated by a number of anti-loyalist journals: *Urdu-i-Mu'alla,* founded in 1906 and edited by Hasrat Mohani, the *Muslim Gazette* of Wahiduddin Salim, 1910, and *Zamindar* of Zafar Ali Khan.

As the old leadership began to recede into the background, a new group of professional men and the *ulama* emerged. They stood for cooperation with Congress and far less reliance on the government.[5] Amongst the *ulama*, Azad and Shibli were forceful advocates of rapprochement with Congress. Azad was highly critical of Western imperialism which he considered both aggressive and anti-Islamic.[6] In relation to India, he cited the instance of the Prophet Mohammad's covenant with some Jews in A.D. 622 as a historical precedent to justify Hindu-Muslim cooperation. He esta-

4 This development was noted by J.S. Meston, Lieutenant-Governor of the United Provinces. He summed up the strength of pro-Congress feelings among Muslims and the declining influence of 'conservative Muslims' in a note submitted to the Viceroy on 7 February 1917. Meston Papers (17).

5 In March 1915, Meston offered an interesting analysis of how the professional men and the *ulama* came to terms with each other. According to him, the 'young educated Muslims are restless and dissatisfied with everybody. His quest is for a cause, a call, something that he can be proud of, something which at small cost will retrieve his self-esteem and restore the glories of his race. This he finds in his religion. It gives him a link with great traditions. It may not be an ethical bond, but it is a militant bond. At this point he comes into touch with the priest of the arrogant domineering type, whose ambition lies in swaying the passions of the ignorant masses. Hence arises Pan-Islamism, the idea of the Muslim 'nation' and many of the fantasies generated from it'. Meston to Hardinge, 25 March 1915, Hardinge Papers (89).

6 *Al-Hilal*, 9 October 1914.

blished, by citations from the Quran, *Hadith*, and the jurists' digests, that joining in common action with one category of non-Muslims, the Hindus, against another category of non-Muslims, the British, was an obligation upon every individual Muslim. Furthermore, Azad urged his co-religionists to join the country's struggle for independence and tried to allay fears of Hindu domination. Such fears, according to him, were deliberately planted by the British government in order to enlist Muslim support for consolidating its rule in India.[7]

The inspiration for these views was most probably provided by Shibli who was well known for his scholarly writings on Islamic history, literature, and religion. The only clue to his political views is provided by his articles published in the *Muslim Gazette*, edited by Maulvi Wahiduddin Salim of Lucknow. In these articles, Shibli argued the case for cooperation with Congress and criticised the League for pursuing sectional and communal policies. He suggested that the League should be freed from the domination of the titled gentry and the *jee-huzoors* so that it could identify itself with the political and economic interests of the country. Shibli observed that in pursuing a comprehensive and constructive economic programme, the Congress, in fact was representing and promoting the best interests of the country.[8]

Similar views were expressed by a group of Western-educated Muslims. Mazharul Haq, who was probably the most respected leader of this group, urged Muslims to join the Congress and referred to 'a great powerful party of liberal Muslims . . . whose aims and ideals are the aims and ideals of the Congress'.[9] The *Comrade*

7 A useful analysis of Azad's role and ideology can be found in Peter Hardy, *Partners in Freedom-and true Muslims: The political thought of some Muslim scholars in British India, 1912-47* (Scandinavian Institute of Asian Studies, 1971).

8 See *Maqalat-i-Shibli* (Azamgarh, 1938), vol. 8, pp. 148-84.

9 *Tribune*, 31 January 1911; *Bengalee*, 27 December 1912.
An intelligence officer summed up the pro-Congress stance of Muslims in north India: 'A reliable correspondent who is clearly in touch with several classes of well-to-do Muslims in the north of India, has informed me that he has not met a single educated Muslim who is not in favour of combination between Muslim politicians in India and the Hindu Congress Party'. WRDCI, 4 July 1912, Home Poll. B, August 1912. Hardinge conceded in August 1913 that his government could not count on the loyalty of Muslims who were prepared to join 'any other faction in opposition to the Raj'. Hardinge to Crewe, 14 August 1913, Hardinge Papers (86).

too, noted the importance of the Congress which embodied the 'genuine and vigorous aspirations which move educated India for a well organised and common national life',[10] and emphasised the need for Hindu-Muslim cooperation. 'It is our firm belief', observed Mohamed Ali, 'that if the Muslims or the Hindus attempt to achieve success in opposition to or even without the cooperation of one another, they will not only fail but fail ignominously'." In the same article, he observed;

> We may not create today the patriotic fervour and fire national frenzy of Japan with its forty millions of homogeneous people. But a concordat like that of Canada is not beyond the bounds of practicability. But a *marrage de convenance* (*sic*), honourably contracted and honourably maintained, is not to be despised.[12]

In another article—'The Communal Patriot'—Mohamad Ali argued that Hindus and Muslims should recognise clearly that there are differences between them which need not interfere with the development of mutual respect. 'None, however, need despair', he wrote, 'as the influences of education, and the levelling, liberalising tendencies of the times are bound to succeed in creating political individuality out of the diversity of creed and race'.[13]

The nationalist aims of the western and the traditionally-educated Muslims, even if impelled by religious motives and prompted by long-term material considerations, provided the *raison d'etre* for cooperation with Congrees and the basis for Hindu-Muslim unity.

II

Mohamed Ali had a profound influence on the changes taking place in Muslim political attitudes. In fact, from the time of the estab-

10 *Comrade*, 30 December 1911.

11 *Ibid.*, p. 822.

12 *Ibid.*

13 *Ibid.*, 10 February 1912. 'Any true patriot of India working for the evolution of Indian nationality', wrote Mohamed Ali, 'will have to accept the common individuality of the Muslims as the basis of his constructive effort'. But he hoped that education and the 'levelling liberalising tendencies' will help in creating 'political individuality out of the diversity of creed and race'.

lishment of the Muslim League in December 1906[14] he was in the centre of every melee, as reformer and social radical, as crusader for the Turkish cause, and as champion of Muslim political interests. In 1912 he was one of the principal organisers of the Medical Mission sent to alleviate the suffering of Turkey in the Balkan War. In 1913 he presented the Muslim version of the Kanpur mosque affair in England, and found an opportunity to address a gathering in Essex Hall about British injustices in India, the anti-Turkish bias of Britain, and the short-sightedness of British colonial policy. That same year he supported Abdul Bari, Shaukat Ali and M.H. Kidwai in the organisation of the *Anjuman-i-Khuddam-i-Ka'aba* in order to maintain the inviolability of the Holy Places.

It is clear from Mohamed Ali's activities that he acted where others doubted or reasoned. In fact, his was a many faceted mind, any one of those facets would have made the reputation of a lesser man. His asset was that he possessed to the full the resources of traditional oratory—its repertoire of tricks. Few orators or political journalists among his contemporaries had his combination of qualities : his range of articulate emotions, his capacity for analytical argument, his pathos, fantasy and wit and his power to marshall all these, through a command over the resources of the language, towards ends clearly discerned and passionately desired. He also had considerable poetic talent, which combined with his fervour and the desperate situation in which Turkey found herself after the war, to create in him a feeling of impending martyrdom.[15] 'Such sufferings and privations as ours', he wrote, 'have only too often been the lot of mankind, in all ages and climes'.[16]

Mohamed Ali's fame spread far and wide when the British put him and his brother in jail on 15 May 1915, for an article on the 'Choice of the Turks'.[17] 'It was Friday and both the brothers had

14 Afzal Iqbal and Shan Muhammed provide some of the details, but their accounts are mainly based on Mohamed Ali's own claims. Government reports, however, bear testimony to the active role of Mohamed Ali.

15 Mujeeb, *Indian Muslims*, p. 537.

16 Mohamed Ali to James DuBoulay, 18 February 1919, MAP.

17 According to W.H. Wheeler, the article 'Choice of the Turks' gave the government 'ample justification for suppressing such writings'. In a note submitted to the Legislative Department (6.10.1914), he observed; 'I do not see how anyone can read the article except as a direct incitement to Turkey to go to war, and practically what it says is that if this does bring them up against Russia and France, they have no cause to love these Powers and it

gone to the Juma Masjid to say their prayers. On that day many thousands of people had congregated in the said mosque to offer their prayers and to bid adieu to the two patriots who had done all they could, to promote their cause'. The official justification of the arrest was offered by the Viceroy. He informed the Secretary of State that

> Mohamed Ali leaves trouble where ever he goes. Recently, he was in Lahore and addressed the students in the Medical College, the result being that a few days later, 14 or 15 students went off to Afghanistan nominally to raise the tribes against us. Mohamed Ali also went to Aligarh College and created trouble, the result being that the Lieutenant-Governors of the Punjab and United Provinces asked the Government of India to prevent these two agitators from entering their provinces. This was, in my opinion, sufficient reason for their internment.[18]

The Ali Brothers were well on their way towards martyrdom. Indeed, government's hasty and harsh decision enabled their

does not matter much. England is practically threatened if she does not evacuate Egypt, and Germany is extolled. If this is not attacking our allies and siding with our enemies it is difficult to know what it is?'. Home Poll. A, October 1913, 142-49, NAI. The Ali Brothers, however, maintained that they were interned 'because we freely expressed and promoted a sympathy, and maintained an allegiance demanded from us by our Islamic faith'. To Viceroy, 24 April 1919, MAP. The Ali Brothers were interned originally at Mehrauli under the Defence of India Act and were transferred subsequently to Lansdowne and, finally, to Chhindwara on 23 November 1915 where they arrived wearing 'grey astrakhan cap with large Turkish half moons in the front, also Khuddam-i-Ka'aba badges'. The decision to transfer them 'to a considerable distance from their friends' and 'far removed from centres of Muhammadan feeling' was taken after much deliberation. The choice fell on Chhindwara because 'Pan-Islamism is faintest' and 'the journey there from the United Provinces as regards visitors is exceedingly tedious'. See Home Poll. D, Proceedings, October 1915, NAI; Home Poll. D, Proceedings, December 1915, 6, NAI.

18 Quoted in Iqbal, *Life and Times*, p. 113. In May 1915, the Ali Brothers, at the orders of Hailey, Chief Commissioner of Delhi, were asked to remain in Mehrauli and to abstain from all meetings of a political nature. They were described by Richard Burn (writing for Meston), as 'disseminators of mischief and would-be-traitors. They have done any amount of evil at Aligarh. They have tried to stir up trouble in Lucknow and their message is mischievous where ever they go'. Home Poll. D, Proceedings, May 1915, 36, NAI.

followers to use the issue of their internment as a lever to stir up a vigorous agitation. Organisations formed in different parts of the country campaigned for the release of a selfless crusader, while friends and political comrades recalled his 'noble services rendered at the most psychological moment in the history of the community.'[19] An address presented to the Ali Brothers revealed the community's perception of their role, particularly that of the younger brother. It stated :

> It would require a volume to enumerate in detail your services in regard to the M.A.O. College, the Muslim University, the galvanising of the Muslim community through your brilliant newspapers, the *Comrade* and the *Hamdard*. . . .the raising of funds for Muslim victims in the Balkan War, the organising of a competent and well-equipped medical mission for the Turkish wounded. Your restoration to liberty is a mark of profound rejoicing to us. . . .Your presence in our midst will stimulate our community into the solidarity seriously imperilled during the last five years of agonizing ordeal.[20]

Impressed with the widespread excitement generated by the internment of the Ali Brothers, leading Congressmen also took up the cause of their release to strengthen the Congress-League *entente* of December 1916. B.G. Tilak, who had played a key role during the Congress-League negotiations in the winter of 1916, introduced a resolution at the Calcutta Congress demanding the release of the Ali Brothers.[21] In October 1917, Annie Besant went to Simla, after her condititional release from internment, with the intention of discussing the same question with the Viceroy. Her aim was to strengthen her alliance with the Muslims, 'who hitherto have been indifferent or hostile to her pretensions'.[22]

It was Gandhi, however, who was the most active campaigner for the release of the Ali Brothers. He had worked with Muslims in South Africa and, after his return to India, was keen to establish

19 Letter issued by Mazharul Haq, M.A. Ansari, 3 September 1917, Khwaja Papers, NML; also, Ansari to A.M. Khwaja, 3 September 1917, *ibid*.

20 *Leader*, 12 and 15 January 1920.

21 *Bombay Chronicle*, 31 December 1917.

22 Willingdon to Chelmsford, 28 October 1917, Willingdon Papers, MSS. EUR. F. 93 (1), IOL.

contacts with Muslim leaders. He met the Ali Brothers in Aligarh and Delhi in 1915, and early in 1916.[23] He attempted to see them in the Chhindwara prison, but was not permitted to do so by the government. 'The authorities have evidently failed', he wrote to Mohamed Ali, 'to appreciate my motive in wanting to see you. The only thing I as a passive resister can do in circumstances such as this is to bow to the decision of the government of India'.[24] On 31 December 1917, Gandhi assured delegates at the Muslim League session held in Calcutta that Hindus were with them to a man in their just struggle for the Ali Brothers' release.[25] On 1 January 1918, he urged the Viceroy to release them, arguing that the Ali Brothers were loyal to the Raj and that their internment was causing great bitterness in India among both Hindus and Muslims. At the same time, he asked for 'definite assurances about Mohammedan States', before lending his support to the loyalty resolution of the Delhi War Conference. But the Viceroy paid no heed to his requests. So, in July 1918, the Mahatma announced his decision to 'engage the government in a duel' on the issue.[26] 'The fight for Mohamed Ali's release is a crushing burden', he wrote, 'though, I know it has but to be borne'.[27] He went on to assure Bi Amma—'Mataji'—that he was 'leaving no stone unturned to secure quick but perfectly honourable release'.[28]

Gandhi attached great significance to his relations with Mohamed Ali because he wanted to secure his cooperation in advancing Hindu-Muslim unity, having made it an essential part of his mission to India since his return from Africa in 1915[29]. 'My interest in

23 Gandhi's relations with the Muslims after his return from South Africa have been adequately discussed by Brown and Robinson.

24 Gandhi to Mohamed Ali, 14 April 1916, MAP. A senior government official reported that Mohamed Ali 'proposes to receive a visit from M.K. Gandhi of South African fame', and enquired whether 'the Government of India desire that Mr. Gandhi should be prohibited from coming to see Mohamed Ali'. Slocock to Wheeler, 17 March 1916, Home Poll. D, Proceedings, March 1918, 38, NAI.

25 *The Collected Works of Mahatma Gandhi* (CWG), vol. 14, p. 120.

26 Gandhi to Maffey, 12 July, 1918, Chelmsford Papers, MSS. EUR. E. 264 (21), IOL.

27 *Day-To-Day with Gandhi* (Varanasi, 1968), vol. 1, p. 93.

28 *Ibid.*, p. 211.

29 'After my arrival in India', Gandhi told a Khilafat meeting, 'I began to find out good Mohammedan leaders. My desire was satisfied when I

your release', the Mahatma wrote to Mohamed Ali, 'is quite selfish. We have a common goal and I want to utilise your services to the uttermost in order to reach that goal. In the proper solution of the Mohammedan question lies the realisation of Swaraj'.[30] He was convinced that self-government could only be achieved if the Hindus and Muslims worked together; so he devoted his energies towards securing 'permanent unity' between them. The distress caused by the Khilafat issue, he said, gave him 'such an opportunity of uniting Hindus and Mohammedans as would not arise in a hundred years'. His inner voice told him that the two communities would unite as brothers one day because there was 'no other course open to them and they have but to be brothers'.

Gandhi assumed that Mohamed Ali, being a representative of Muslim opinion, was an ideal instrument in his hand for creating Hindu-Muslim alliance with the aim of obtaining Swaraj. Because to Gandhi Swaraj meant not just political Home Rule but a state of communal harmony, Mohamed Ali was valuable to him both as an issue on which to cement a communal alliance, and also because he thought that he was a splendid example of that mingling of Hindu and Muslim culture which had occurred in the U.P.[31]

Gandhi's efforts bore fruit. His initiatives in connection with the release of the Ali Brothers earned him the popularity and adulation of many leading Muslims. M.A. Ansari extolled him as the 'intrepid leader of India . . . who has . . . endeared him as much to the Musalman as to the Hindu'.[32] His non-violent programme was endorsed by Mohamed Ali and his younger colleagues who regarded the Mahatma as a 'Tolstoy and Buddha combined'.[33] There was similar enthusiasm for the passive resistance movement launched against the Rowlatt Bills. Satyagraha, declared Abdul

reached Delhi, and found the Brothers Ali, whom I had the privilege of knowing before. It was a question of love at first sight between us. When I met Dr. Ansari, the circle of Mohammedan friends widened at last it even included Maulana Abdul Bari'. Speech on Khilafat, Bombay, 9 May 1919, *CWG*, vol. 15, p. 295.

30 Gandhi to Mohamed Ali, 18 November 1918, *ibid.*, p. 64.

31 This paragraph is based on Brown, *Gandhi's Rise to Power*, p. 152.

32 Speech delivered by Ansari at Muslim League Session in December 1918, quoted in Mushirul Hasan (ed.), *Muslims and the Congress : Select Correspondence of Dr. M.A. Ansari* (Delhi, 1979), appendix I.

33 Abdur Rahman Siddiqi to Mohamed Ali, 24 March 1919, MAP.

Bari, the renowned *alim* of Firangi Mahal in Lucknow, was quite in accord with Islamic principles.[34]

Gandhi's influence was not confined to the *ulama* or the western-educated Muslims, but extended to Muslim artisans, merchants, millworkers and weavers, who participated in the *hartal* organised on 6 April 1919. His success in securing their adherence was due to two main reasons. First, Gandhi was able to exploit the resentment nursed against the British government's policy towards the Khalifa of Turkey. He also succeded in arousing Muslim support for the satyagraha amidst rumours that the Rowlatt Bills were intended to coerce the Muslims and prevent them from giving trouble so as to facilitate the dismemberment of Turkey. Secondly, the economic distress flowing from the First World War also accounted for the favourable response to Gandhi's call for satyagraha. During and after the war there was a sharp increase in the prices of basic commodities such as rice, wheat, salt and cooking oil. In the U.P. because of lack of rain, foodgrain production fell sharply and large areas of the province were hit by famine or scarcity. The province, like other regions of India, was affected by the great influenza which caused the death of at least five to six million people. It was the astute organisational leadership of Gandhi which enabled him to canalise these local discontents into a movement of protest against the government. The discontent engendered by the Rowlatt Act acted as 'a touchstone for a variety of grievances that would have otherwise remained quiescent'.[35] 'Khilafat', 'Swaraj', 'Gandhi', 'Mohamed Ali', were all words to conjure up in the minds of the people a picture of bringing about a better world under the direction of better leaders.[36]

III

In spite of his involvement in the pan-Islamic agitation, Mohamed Ali reaffirmed his attachment to the Raj and commented on the

34 WRDCI, March 1919, Home Poll. B, April 1919, 148-52, NAI; Also see Daryabadi, *Za'ati Diary*, p. 20.

35 D.W. Ferrell, 'The Rowlatt Satyagraha in Delhi', in Ravinder Kumar (ed.), *Essays on Gandhian Politics: The Rowlatt Satyagraha of 1919* (Oxford, 1971), p. 212.

36 W.J. Watson, 'Muhammad Ali and the Khilafat Movement' (Unpublished M.A. thesis, McGill University, 1955) p. 62.

good that was to accrue to India from the beneficent contact: 'the impulses for wholesome national life, which a contact with western culture, has called forth amongst the Indian mind want a home for a full, many-sided expression'.[37] The Muslims, he made it plain in his articles, were not completely satisfied with their position, but it was the social distinction between the races rather than the fact of British rule that distressed them.

Mohamed Ali's relations with British officials were cordial. High-ranking British officers subscribed to the *Comrade* when it began publication, because they desired to see some one speak up for the Muslims and against the Hindus.[38] Hardinge, in particular, pampered Mohamed Ali, allowed him to collect and advance a loan to Turkey, patronised the Delhi Crescent Society, and extended support to his brainchild—the Medical Mission to Constantinople.[39]

Such friendly overtures were duly reciprocated by Mohamed Ali. In his correspondence with Dunlop Smith, James Meston and F.H. Lucas, he adopted a conciliatory tone,expressed his profound loyalty to the government, and reaffirmed his support to its policies. 'I shall . . . try', he assured Meston, 'my best to run up to Aligarh when you are there and to confirm once more what I have said before as to my anxious desire to cooperate with you and every well-wisher of my country and community in working for their progress'.[40]

The desire to cooperate with the British is best reflected in his temperate criticism of the annulment of Bengal's partition in 1911, an issue which otherwise engendered widespread disaffection amongst Muslims. It is generally not known that Mohamad Ali made no contribution to the intense debate on the question. On the contrary, he pleaded with the Director of Intelligence for 'some pegs' on which to hang the moderation of his stance.[41] The significance of

37 Quoted in *ibid.*, p. 14.

38 Mujeeb, *Indian Muslims*, p. 537.

39 The correspondence with the Viceroy on these issues is in Hardinge Papers (84); Iqbal, *Life and Times*, pp. 77-78.

40 Mohamed Ali to Meston, 19 February 1913, MAP.

41 Quoted in Neelam Malhotra,, The Khilafat Movement in Delhi: A Socio-Political Study of Delhi Muslims, 1912-1927' (Unpublished M. Phil. thesis, Delhi University, 1981), p. 64.
Mohamed Ali, reported DuBoulay, 'talked very reasonably and said that

this plea was most clearly articulated in his suggestion to James DuBoulay. "Well-merited concessions wisely made at a suitable moment', he insisted, 'would prevent such an agitation far more effectively than the most strenuous efforts of the leaders of Muslim opinion'.[42] In an attempt to drive home his point, Mohamed Ali also wrote to F.H. Lucas. 'It is impossible to disguise the fact', he argued, 'that for obvious reasons Muslim feeling in India is far from normal today. I would, therefore, respectfully suggest that the presence of His Majesty in India at this juncture should be fully utilised to restore its equilibrium to the feeling, and to bind still more firmly the seventy million Muslims of India to the Throne and Person of His Majesty. In my humble judgement it would be an infinite pity if such a great opportunity is lost through any avoidable delay, even if the delay is caused by the need of greater deliberation'.[43]

This is not all. Even when Mohamed Ali was snubbed and ignored, as was the case during his stay in London from September to November 1913, he maintained his cool, trying to convince the British government 'of the essential loyalty of the Muslim community to His Majesty's person and throne',[44] and 'our sense of appreciation of the manifold blessings of British rule in India'.[45] When the War with Germany broke out, Mohamad Ali found himself on the side of the British, urging the Turks not to participate in the War and his community to 'place their services at the disposal of the Government for the preservation of peace and tranquility in India.[46] The article—*The Choice of the Turks*—likewise proclaimed

he always made a point of making the most of any government action favouring Muslim aspiration'. Also, Mohamed Ali was quite ready to listen, but argued that 'he must have some peg on which to hang any modification of his tone. A sudden change wtthout any reason would . . . defeat its own ends, for people would say he had been got at and was looking for an honour. . .' J.H. DuBoulay to Reginald Craddock, 9 February 1913, Hardinge Papers (85).

42 Mohamed Ali to James DuBoulay, 3 January 1912, MAP.

43 Mohamed Ali to F.H. Lucas, 3 January 1912, *ibid.*

44 Statement, *Comrade*, 13 September 1913.

45 Mohamed Ali to James LaTouche, 4 November 1913, Mohamed Ali to T.W. Holderness, 13 November 1913, Crewe Papers, CUL. Also see appendix.

46 Evidence on Mohamed Ali's support for the Raj during the war is in the works of Afzal Iqbal, Shan Muhammad, and Watson.

the hope that the Khalifa would stay out of the war and so save Indian Muslims from a conflict of loyalties. It is therefore not surprising that Ansari held the view: 'why the youngmen in Delhi did not turn to extremist nationalism, was the influence of constitutional agitators like Mohamed Ali'.[47]

IV

Mohamed Ali went to Europe whenever he could, to renew himself, as he said, and because it revived his hopes that the Muslim world would recover from its present state. In the course of his mission in 1913, he met and spoke with writers, journalists, scientists and only a few civil servants. Such an opportunity enabled him to see Turkey from the outside, to observe the factious strife of the peninsula magnified into the terms of international politics, to watch and appraise the forces remoulding, sometimes deliberately, sometimes almost casually, the destiny of the Ottoman Empire. This 'diplomatic experience' was important in another respect; it influenced Mohamed Ali's views on the role of government *vis-a-vis* the Muslims. Having once regarded the British as the safe custodian of Muslim interests, he now began to perceive their role differently. 'British politicians, journalists, authors, and even ministers', he wrote angrily, 'are hopelessly ignorant about conditions in India, and their ignorance is driving them fast to the brink of the precipice'.[48] Echoing his sentiments, as indeed of many of his co-religionists, Mohamed Ali wrote that 'the Muslims felt themselves to be betrayed both in India and abroad and in being their spokesman I soon lost grace with the official world'.[49] He was particularly bitter because his endeavour to explain the purpose of his mission was thwarted by suspicious and cynical officials both in Delhi and in London; he was indeed refused an interview with the Secretary of State and other leading members at the India House. 'If we are unable to see even His Lordship', Mohamed Ali complained to John Morley, 'what could we say to our people on our return except that because some local officials were desirous that we and our co-religionists and many others in our country should be mis-

47 Malhotra, *op. cit.*, p. 64.
48 Mohamed Ali to O.M. Edwards, 14 November 1913, Crewe Papers.
49 *My Life: A Fragment*, p. 35.

judged by our superiors'.[50] Such an experience shattered his faith and confidence in the Raj, a fact which also contributed to his estrangement from unsympathetic British officials. Furious at their lack of sensitivity, he was drawn into a kind of *egoisme a deux* in defying their stuffiness. 'Muslim loyalty and support', he wrote some years later,

> had so often been assured to Government in our generation, and even Muslim contentment was so often unduly taken for granted, that other communities had with some justice made our attitude towards Government almost a matter of reproach. It was strange for all this loyalty and support that, without any effective protest, and often with the concurrence of His Majesty's Government, blow after blow was aimed at the temporal power of Islam.[51]

Mohamed Ali's internment in 1915 was the last proverbial straw.[52] From his cell in Mehrauli, Chhindwara, Lansdowne and Betul, he wrote endless letters condemning government and its repressive measures. He was particularly harsh on the Indian Civil Service, 'a political party perpetually in office (with) the power to crush its political opponents with all the resources of the State', and all the 'pillars of the party of privilege'—James Meston, Michael O'Dwyer, Reginald Craddock, Charles Clevaland, and Malcolm Hailey—who 'hate me with a malignant hate'.[53] 'I was not much surprised at your order of internment', he wrote to Malcolm Hailey on 24 May 1915, 'because I have known something of the official mind for a good many years, and I can understand how hateful must be a man of my character to officials of a certain type. I also know the all comprehensive character of the Defence of India Act which makes even the Archangel Gabriel liable to internment by local governments on the secret testimony of Beelzebub'.[54] A month later, he declared: 'We consider the

50 Mohamed Ali to John Morley, 2 November 1913, MAP.

51 Mohamed Ali to Chelmsford, 24 April 1919, *ibid*.

52 Ziauddin Ahmad Barni (d 1968), a sub-editor of *Hamdard*, traced Mohamed Ali's anti-government stance to his internment in Chhindwara, 'Maulana Mohamed Ali Jauhar', *Naqqush* (*Shakhsiat* Number), October 1956, p. 1161.

53 Mohamed Ali to Chelmsford, 24 April 1919, MAP.

54 Mohamed Ali to Malcolm Hailey, 24 May 1915, *ibid*.

law under which you purport to have acted as tyrannous and unjust'.[55] To the Vicerory, Mohamed Ali wrote:

> No government was expected in the twentieth century to claim, even by implication, the right to force a man's conscience. And yet it only on this hypothesis that the action of government with respect to the internment of Muslim *ulama* and public workers, and the virtual suppression of the entire Muslim press, culminating in the forfeiture of Dr. Ansari's address, becomes intelligible.[56]

Again,

> the war is now over, but the spirit of tyranny that it generated is still abroad. . . .the government. . . .is denying to the people of India the barest expression of opinion on questions that vitally concern them. Not only is the gag not to be removed yet from our mouths, but a gag of prodigious proportions has been prepared now for silencing more than three hundred million of God's articulate creatures. The Rowlatt Bills, just enacted in the most tyrannical manner, has ended the reign of law, and substituted a reign of terror in its place. . . .[57]

The long and lonely years in prison were a turning point in Mohamed Ali's relationship with government. It was during these years that he discovered the 'evil' character of British rule, recognised the futility of the politics of mendicancy so forcefully advocated by Syed Ahmad Khan, and realised the necessity of agitational methods for the redressal of grievances. This posture was best evident at the Amritsar Congress (1919) where Mohamed Ali appeared as a spokesman of the militant group. His advocacy of the nationalist causes was impressive; so was his unequivocal condemnation of government policies. Indeed, jail had turned Mohamed Ali into a bitter critic of the Raj. As a symbol of his protest, he began to wear half-moons in his grey cap and *Khuddam-i-Ka'aba* badge, compared with his European style of dress in previous years.

55 *Ibid.*, 2 June 1915.
56 Mohamed Ali to Chelmsford, 24 April 1919, *ibid.*
57 *Ibid.*

The enforced leisure was important in another respect; it made Mohamed Ali more deeply religious, enabled him to steep himself afresh in his Islamic heritage and to turn to the study of Islam—charting out an unfamiliar subject, getting at its rudiments, and exploring its nuances. In the seclusion of his internment at Mehrauli, he studied 'at leisure God's Book that we had so long neglected', and found in it 'the consolation and contentment that was denied to us outside its pages'.[58] The main tenets of Islam which had earlier seemed to be 'little more than a bundle of doctrines and commandments' now acquired 'a new coherence and, as it were, fell suddenly into place, creating an effect of units such as I had never realised before'.[59] Again, it was during those years of enforced inactivity that Mohamed Ali read *Sihah-i-Sittah*, a compilation of the Prophet's Traditions (*hadith*), and the works of Imam Ghazali, Shibli Nomani, T.W. Arnold, and the poetry of Jalaluddin Rumi and Mohammad Iqbal. The reading of *Asrar-i-Khudi*, (Secrets of Self) was a delightful experience. 'I experienced an exquisite thrill of delight', he wrote, 'when I found that the Poet and Philosopher was, in his own unimitable fashion giving expression to the self-same basic truth of Islam, which I had in a blundering sort of way discovered for myself'.[60] Such readings enabled him to discover both the dogmas and ethical codes of his religion and the strong links which bounded Muslims throughout the world. He also realized the significance of the disintegration of the Muslim states in the history of Islam, and the need for Indian Muslims to identify themselves with the declining fortunes of their brother-Muslims everywhere in the world. Above all, on turning to the study of Islamic history, Mohamed Ali saw its great men as figures to whom he could talk, and its crises as guides to action in current affairs.[61] The study of Islam was conventional enough for many of his contemporaries; men like Abul Kalam Azad studied it with greater scholarship, but none with a greater personal need. Mohamed Ali recalled :

Since I first commenced the study of the Quran I have read a

58 *My Life: A Fragment*, pp. 63, 77, 85-6.

59 *Ibid.*, p. 88.

60 *Ibid.*, p. 80.

61 See Daryabadi, *Za'ati Diary*, p. 14; Mohamed Ali to A.M. Daryabadi, 22 May, 25 July 1916 (Urdu), Daryabadi Papers NML; see appendix.

fair amount about Islam from the point of view of Muslims and also of their critics; *but nothing that I have read has altered the significance of Islam for me to which I had stumbled in the first few months of our internment eight years ago* (emphasis added).[62]

To Gandhi, he wrote :

> . . .Whatever else my internment may or may not have done, it has I believe set the soul free, and that compensates me for so many items on the wrong side of the account. What I could dimly perceive before I now realise with distinctness, and it is this, that the whole aim and end of life is to serve God and obey His commandments. . . .I confess I had never before grasped this truth in all its fullness . . . . *.Internment made us seek refuge in the Holy Quran, and for the first time, I have to confess it, I read it through and with new eyes* (emphasis added). It was then that this truth dawned upon me and gave me coherence and a unity to a thousand vague aspirations to do good to my people, my country and men and women in general.[63]

This religious fervour characterised the rest of his life. His earlier activities had been directed by communal loyalty, but after his religious experience his motivation was Islamic duty. This is not to suggest that he held his community in any lesser esteem, or that its mundane welfare was any less important to him. On the contrary, his awakening confirmed the rightness of what he had been doing in the past, and made it necessary for him to intensify his endeavours along identical lines.[64]

62 *My Life*: *A Fragment*, p. 18.

63 Mohamed Ali to Gandhi, 20 February 1918, MAP.

64 Watson, *op. cit.* Watson has argued that Mohamed Ali's loyalty to Islam was expressed in the days before the Turko-Italian War as loyalty to the Indian Muslim Community rather than to an abstract way to Allah. His communal consciousness, as he said, was far more secular than religious: his decision to take to journalism was dictated by the 'secular affairs of my country' rather than by a 'religious call'. Then, in the seclusion of his internment, he read through the Quran in Urdu. Islam possessed him and he discovered the dogmas and ethical codes of his religion. After this experience, argues Watson, his motivation was 'Islamic duty' rather than 'communal loyalty'.

3

THE KHILAFAT AND NON-COOPERATION MOVEMENTS: FULFILMENT OF A MISSION*

There can be no doubt that the Indian Muslims, who share a set of common beliefs and practices with their brethren elsewhere, have been acutely aware of their fraternal links with the world of Islam. This was reflected in the *Mussadas* of Altaf Husain Hali, in Mohammad Iqbal's nostalgic ode to once-Arab Sicily, and in Shibli Numani's 'wistful and pungent' *Trouble in the Balkans*; in the "Movement in favour of Islamic Culture of the Past" led by Ameer Ali, Shibli and Abdul Halim Sharar, and in the pan-Islamic proclivities of Abul Kalam Azad, Maulana Mahmud al-Hasan, Mohamed Ali, Ajmal Khan, Ubaid-Allah Sindhi, M.A. Ansari, and Maulana Abdul Bari.

For most Muslims, however, the overriding consideration was that the Sultan of Turkey was the custodian and defender of the Holy Places in the area known as *Jazirat al-Arab*. The impending danger to the sanctuaries and symbols of Islam—central to Muslim belief and practice—caused deep anguish leading the faithful to demand that the *Jazirat al-Arab* remain under Muslim sovereignty according to the injunctions of the Prophet and the Khalifa should continue to be its warden. In fact, the protection of the Holy

* In writing this chapter, I have made use of the thesis of Watson. His study, though primarily based on secondary sources, provides some useful insights into the progress of the Khilafat movement in general, and the role of Mohamed Ali, in particular. The works of Shan Muhammad and Afzal Iqbal, on the other hand, are analytically poor. Their explanation of Mohamed Ali's pan-Islamic concerns is both conventional and lacking in analytical rigour.

Places rather than the preservation of the tottering Turkish Empire provided the rallying point for virtually all sections of the Muslim community. Money and ornaments poured into the Khilafat Fund and thousands of enthusiasts flocked to the Khilafat meetings to voice their deep concern and uneasiness over the safety and preservation of the Holy Places. Many left the fields and factories to migrate to the *dar al-Islam* in response to a call for *hijrat;* students abandoned their studies and joined the swelling ranks of non-cooperators; and many others gave up their lucrative jobs and high-sounding titles. Never before did so many Muslims unite on a common platform to fight a common cause. It was a unique example of their solidarity.

In order to provide organisational expression to Muslim sentiments, a Khilafat Committee was founded in March 1919 which aimed to secure not only a just and honourable peace for Turkey, but also the fulfilment of the pledges given by the British Prime Minister, Lloyd George. The next important stage in the development of the Khilafat movement was the observance of 19 March as Khilafat Day; and on that day Gandhi, who had gone further than most Hindus in public life to work with Muslims, announced that he would launch a non-cooperation movement if the Turkish peace treaty did not satisfy the Indian Muslims. Accordingly, when the peace terms were announced in May 1920, the All-India Khilafat Committee adopted Gandhi's non-cooperation programme. On 2 June, at Gandhi's suggestion, a conference of all parties was held at Allahabad which decided upon a policy of non-cooperation and appointed a committee to draw up a programme. On 1 August, the Khilafat Committee organised a *hartal* and entrusted Gandhi with the leadership of the Non-cooperation movement. Gandhi launched the movement by surrendering his titles and decorations to the government. 'Valuable as these honours have been to me', he wrote to the Viceroy, 'I cannot wear them with an easy conscience so long as my Mussalman countrymen have to labour under wrong done to their religious sentiments'.[1]

1 Gandhi to Viceroy, 2 August 1920, Home Poll. Deposit, August 1920, 38, NAI.

II

Mohamed Ali's emotional disposition in religious matters had surely much to do with the nature and with the promptness of his response to events in Turkey. In this context there is no reason at all to doubt the sincerity of his indignation, aroused by the machinations of some European Powers, and his genuinely-felt emotional concern for the safety of the Holy Places. The opinion, presented by Francis Robinson and others, that it was all feigned, that he was simply playing the pan-Islamist, cannot be seriously defended. Calculation comes in, not in pretending an emotion which is not there, but in deciding how much of a genuinely-felt emotion to release publicly; how far to let oneself go.[2] Similarly, it is difficult to sustain the charge, rendered plausible by Mohamed Ali's complicated financial situation, that he lived off the Khilafat Fund. Such an allegation was inspired by Mohamed Ali's detractors, especially amongst government officials, the landlords, and a section of the *ulama*.

Mohamed Ali's pan-Islamism was not instinctive, but the outcome of much thought and deliberation. Central to his belief was the view, based on the concept of *umma*, that 'the basis of Islamic sympathy is not a common domicile or common parentage, but a common outlook on life and common culture' and that 'the embodiment of that culture is the Khilafat'. Inspired by Abul Kalam Azad's description of a 'political centre' (*siyasi markaz*), Mohamed Ali argued that the 'personal centre' of Islam was the Khalifa and the 'local centre' was the 'island of Arabia', the *Jazirat al-Arab.*

> So no part of the territories included in the expression *Jazirat al-Arab* should be directly or indirectly occupied or subjugated to any form of non-Muslim control, but must remain under independent Muslim occupation and control, as required by the testamentary injunction of the Prophet.[3]

He regarded the protection of the Holy Places of Islam as a religious duty, 'a duty more sacred than any other', and warned the government that

2 This idea is borrowed from the brilliant introduction by Conor Cruise O'Brien to *Reflections on the Revolution in France* (London, 1969 edn.).

3 Home Poll. July 1925, 155, NAI.

> there should be no attempt to remove, whether directly or indirectly, from the independent, indivisible and inalienable sovereignty of the Khalifa, who is the recognised servant of the Holy Places and warden of the Holy Shrines, any portion of the territories in which such Holy Places and Shrines are situated . . . .Nor should there be any such attempt to dismember and parcel out even among Muslim Governments, or in any other manner weaken the Khalifa's Empire with the object of weakening the temporal power of Islam, and thereby make it liable to suffer, without adequate power to prevent, the curtailment of its spiritual influence through the temporal power of other creeds.[4]

It was not merely ceremonial piety that motivated Mohamed Ali and other Khilafatists to rally under the Khilafat banner. The Khalifa, according to the classical theorists, was the Defender of the Faith and weilded authority to ensure that Muslims follow the *sharia*. For this reason, the Khilafat was 'the most essential institution of the Muslim community', and its defence was a sacred duty.[5] Mohamed Ali gave the need for preserving in the institution a utilitarian quality when he told a London audience:

> Well, so long as there are your Bryces and your "Big Sticks", we, too, must have some sort of stick for the defence of our faith, and to jeopardise at least the dominance of those that jeopardise the freedom of our conscience. That, and that alone is the *rationale* of our main claim that the Khilafat should be preserved with adequate temporal power.[6]

He also took great pains to explain that Muslims were not concerned with political dominance because the 'spiritual force of Islam' did not depend on political supremacy. What concerned them most was the weakening of the temporal power of Islam to the extent that it might become 'liable to suffer, without adequate power to prevent, the curtailment of its spiritual influence through the pressures of the temporal power of rival creeds'.[7]

4 Mohamed Ali to Chelmsford, 24 April 1919; also, see his speech delivered in London on 22 April 1920, quoted in Iqbal (ed.), *Writings and Speeches*, pp. 183-193.

5 'India's Message to France', *ibid.*, p. 158; also, *Comrade*, 13 May 1913.

6 'A People's right to Live', *ibid.*, p. 171.

7 Mohamed Ali to Chelmsford, 24 April 1919, MAP.

The defence of the Khalifa and the Holy Places was seen as the method of assuring that the *ummat-i-Islamia* be given the freedom to conform to its religious precepts. The Khilafatists envisioned a renascent Islamic world, in which all Muslim peoples were united in a strong Islamic world—'the Supernatural Sangathan of Muslims in Five Continents'[8]—built around the Khalifa and supporting each other through that institution whenever there was a threat to the security of any Muslim.[9] The new Khalifa, judged from the views expressed by Mohamed Ali at the Mecca Conference in 1928, would be based on the pattern of the *Khilafat-i-Rashida.* It would be a democratic institution, elective rather than dynastic, and the holder of the office would be chosen by virtue of his godliness, his devotion to Islam. All the Muslims of the world would have part in the direction of the government, all would be responsible for its welfare. This was a romantic vision, but Mohamed Ali was not one to recognise the dramatic changes in the 'Islamic world', the emergence of nationalism as a force, and the rejection of pan-Islamic ideals in most countries, including Turkey. He continued to picture a new Muslim world—unified by common religious symbols and experiences—which would present a single force to whatever power attempted to jeopardise the rights of any Muslim. The Indian Muslims, the largest single community in the Islamic world, would provide the leadership in the fight to emancipate Islam.[10]

III

The realization of the ideal of a renascent Islam demanded serious organizational efforts, a systematic mobilization campaign, and the active support of various Muslim groups, particularly the *ulama.* The Khilafat Committees were pressed into service to preach the gospel of pan-Islamism and to draw a wide spectrum of the commu-

8 Mohamed Ali observed: 'Islam united Muslims by offering a set of common ideals and offered the only rational basis for unity and cooperation among its followers. The sympathies of a Muslim are co-extensive with his religion because they have been bred into him by the inspiring spirit of his creed'. *Comrade*, 12 April 1913.

9 Watson, *op. cit.*, p. 55.

10 *Ibid.*

nity into the movement; so were the newspapers which focussed on the declining fortunes of Muslim States and served to heighten the pan-Islamic consciousness of the common people. Contacts were also established with the *ulama* and with their leading educational centres—the *Dar al-ulum* at Deoband, the Firangi Mahal and the *Nadvat al-ulama* in Lucknow. They were invited to meetings and conferences in order to add weight to the Khilafat demands, and leaders like Abdul Bari and Maulvi Kifayatullah were given a prominent place on the platform.[11]

The *ulama* responded favourably to such overtures, mainly because they were politically unorganised and indeed unaccustomed to political life. Moreover, their bitter doctrinal disputes and mutual rivalries created fissures in the apparent solid phalanx of orthodoxy and prevented them from moving in unison to defend their interests.[12] By 1911, however, the *ulama* were rudely awakened by the growing threat to Islam—an awakening which coincided

11 For details of the alliance between the *ulama* and the western-educated Muslims, see Mushirul Hasan (ed.), *Communal and Pan-Islamic Trends in Colonial India* (Delhi, 1981); Robinson, *Separatism Among Indian Muslims*, chapter seven; Peter Hardy, *The Muslims of British India* (Cambridge, 1972), pp. 182-185.

12 For an insight into the nature of differences, see Robinson, *Separatism Among Indian Muslims*, pp. 268-71. For personal rivalries amongst the *ulama* in Deoband, see Gail Minault, 'The Khilafat Movement: A Study of Indian Muslim Leadership 1919-24' (Unpublished Ph.D thesis, University of Pennsylvania, 1972), pp. 66-70. A number of leading *ulama* kept aloof from the Khilafat and non-cooperation movements and criticised their fellow divines for associating with the Hindus. Maulana Ahmad Raza Khan of Bareilly was one of them. In 1921, he formed the *Jama'at-i-Ansar-ul-Islam* to counter pan-Islamism and convened a conference for that purpose. The first conference of the Jama'at was addressed by Maulana Mohammad Mian (1892-1956) of *Khanqah-i-Barkatia* in Marehra, a small town in Etah district of U.P. The Maulana vigorously opposed the Khilafat agitation, advocated cooperation with the British and denounced the Khilafatists, including Abdul Bari, for associating with Gandhi and other Hindu Congressmen. See S. Jamaluddin 'The Barelvis and the Khilafat Movement', in Hasan (ed.), *Communal and Pan-Islamic Trends*. In Sind, the *pirs* were equally divided. The *pir* of Kingri, for instance, not only opposed non-cooperation but also advised his *murids* to remain loyal to the government. Pir Rashidullah, another influential Muslim divine, held aloof from the movement because it was 'initiated and controlled by Hindus'. WR (Sind), 9 April 1921, J.C. Curry Papers, Centre for South Asian Studies, Cambridge.

with, and was also to a certain extent caused by, the political upheaval in Turkey. They were conscious that they must now be active in addressing themselves to the current anxieties—political, social and religious—of Indian Muslims, or else see true Islam as they understood it, and their own claims to guide the community go by default. Such a realization led some *ulama* to assiduously cultivate the modern-educated Muslims who had some experience of conducting constitutional politics and, in the words of Mohamed Ali, 'to pocket their pride and in a way even accept the lead of men whom they had but a generation ago finally consigned to perdition'.[13] An early move in this direction was initiated by Maulana Mahmud al-Hasan who was convinced of the need to further greater fraternity between the alumni of Deoband and Aligarh. The *Jalsa i-Dastarbandi,* convened in 1910 and attended by a delegation from Aligarh led by Aftab Ahmad Khan, and the *Jamiat al-Ansar*, founded by Ubaid-Allah Sindhi, was the fruition of such endeavours.[14]

These initiatives were followed by the establishment of the *Anjuman-i-Khuddam-i-Ka'aba* in May 1912, an organization for the defence of the Ka'aba, the symbol of the essential unity of all Islamic peoples and, in the words of the poet Mohammad Iqbal, the personification of the Islamic ideal of a single and indivisible nation of the children of Adam. This was the beginning of the generality of the *ulamas*' formal participation in Indian politics in their capacity as religious leaders. The *Anjuman* also provided the basis for an alliance between leading *ulama* of all shades of opinion and the modern-educated. This was of great significance because it illustrated that, on purely religious issues, the *alim* and the modernised Muslim could strive together for common ends. Ideologically, they had little in common, but this did not prevent them from combining against what they commonly perceived as a threat to Islam. The orthodox and the anglicised 'were drawn together and, as in a flash of lightning, saw that after all they were not so unlike each other as they had imagined'.[15] 'Once more',

13 *My Life: A Fragment*, p. 43.

14 Z.H. Faruqi, *The Deoband School and the Demand for Pakistan* (London, 1963), pp. 56-7. Also, see the speech of Mahmud al-Hasan delivered at the foundation of Jamia Millia Islamia in *ibid.*, 65-6.

15 *My Life: A Fragment*, p. 43.

observed Mohamed Ali :

> Muslim society in India presented a level of uniformity and the bitterest opponents of a generation ago stood shoulder to shoulder. . . . .If even a decade previously anyone had ventured to foretell such a result, he would have been laughed at for such a fantastic prophesy. . . .[16]

The annulment of the partition of Bengal, the Turko-Italian War, the furore over the Kanpur mosque affair, and the rejection of the Muslim University scheme added thrust to the converging courses in politics of the modern and the traditionally-educated. 'The temporal misfortunes of Islam, therefore, drew the Muslims to their religion as if inevitably and the wedge that western education seemed to insert between the ranks of the religious, and of the men of the 'New Light' vanished as if by magic', observed Mohamed Ali.[17]

The alliance with the *ulama* and the establishment of organizations like *Anjuman-i-Khuddam-i-Ka'aba* was not enough. It was also necessary to mobilise the Muslim masses and to stimulate their religious consciousness through a newspaper. So the *Hamdard* was launched on 13 June 1913, adding to the growing number of pan-Islamic newspapers in Urdu.[18] Combining this new venture with frequent lectures and deputations was a truly impressive feat. But the government had little cause to remain passive for long; on 15 May 1915, the Ali Brothers, described as 'disseminators of mischief and would-be traitors' were interned in the desolate village at Mehrauli.[19]

IV

Years in prison failed to dampen the spirit of the ebullient Mohamed Ali. Soon after his release on 28 December 1919, he reached

16 *Ibid.*, p. 44. 'A general levelling up has taken place in the Muslim community which had made it a power in the land such as it had never been before, and that, without any dependence on the use of force or external authority'. *Ibid.*, p. 48.

17 *Ibid.*, p. 43.

18 The *Hamdard*, according to Mohamed Ali, 'was intended to educate the people whereas the *Comrade* had to be their spokesman, as well, and to act as a medium between them and their rulers'. *Ibid.*, p. 59.

19 See f.n. 15 in chapter II.

Amritsar where, in keeping with the practice that had developed during the war years, the Indian National Congress and the Muslim League were holding simultaneous meetings. He made two speeches at the conferences. To the Congress he spoke in what might be termed an anti-colonial vein. He had been imprisoned, he said, for denouncing the injustices that had been perpetrated on India and on Islam by the British, and now he must denounce them still, even if it meant returning to prison. The speech made a few hours later to the Muslim League was more concerned with religious issues. He spoke of the omni-supremacy of Allah, both in Heaven and earth, and expressed his readiness to sacrifice every thing he had, including his life, for the sake of Allah and Islam.[20] He also declared that Muslims were subjects of Allah and not of Great Britain and exhorted his audience to defend the Ka'aba at all cost.[21] This was also the burden of his speeches in London where he went as member of the Khilafat Delegation in February 1920.

The delegation arrived in England early in March, and for the next six months maintained an exhausting pace, spurred on, no doubt, by the ardour of Mohamed Ali. Mohamed Ali was the debonair gentlemen, perfectly dressed, dispensing political wisdom, epigrams, jokes and anecdotes to representative British audience, impressing everyone except the imperialist newspapers and Lloyd George—the man who mattered.[22] He lived well 'in a nice flat with heaps of good food, taxis to go about'[23], organised meetings with British leaders, made speeches to various official and non-official bodies, and helped to set up two propaganda organs: the *Moslem Outlook* in England and *Echo de l'Islam* in Paris.

The fate of the Khilafat Delegation was predictable. The publication of the Peace Terms on 14 May 1920 confirmed the worst fears. Under the peace terms, Turkey was to be shorn of its Arab possessions—Syria, Palestine, Mesopotamia, and Hijaz, and other Turkish provinces in the Arab peninsula. The portion of the Asiatic and European shores of the Bosphorus was to be internationalised. The other half, extending from St. Stefano to Dalma Bagtche, was declared a port of international interest under

20 Watson, *op. cit.*, pp. 44-45.

21 P.C. Bamford, *Histories of the Khilafat and Non-cooperation Movements* (Delhi, 1975), Reprint, p. 146.

22 Mujeeb, *Indian Muslims*, p. 537

23 Mohamed Ali to Shaukat Ali, 15 May 1920, MAP.

a Commission on which Turkey was not even represented. In effect, the peace terms proposed to sever from Turkey provinces and districts predominantly inhabited by the Turks, and to impose suzerainty over the Turkish sovereign which, according to the Indian Muslims, would affect his status and prestige as the religious head of the community. Finally, the terms were designed to retain the protectorate of the sacred cities of Islam in non-Muslim hands. So the efforts of the Khilafat Delegation came to nothing. This was not surprising. Their demands did not deserve serious consideration because they were inconsistent with British imperial interests. The *Moslem Outlook* observed:

> Having won, through the sacrifices of their Moslem soldiers, their present position of dominance, the Allies, like the ungrateful monster of Shakespeare, Caliban, now turn round to the Mussalmans and say: "You have given us power and we know how to crush your most cherished religious sentiments".[24]

Gandhi described the peace proposals as a 'staggering blow' to the Indian Muslims and declared non-cooperation as the 'only effective remedy. . . for healing the wounds inflicted on Mohammedan opinion'. There was nothing new in this statement because, on 7 March 1920, Gandhi had already committed himself to non-cooperation as 'the only remedy left open to us'. On 14 March, the Central Khilafat Committee endorsed non-cooperation. In early June, the Joint and Central Khilafat Conferences held in Allahabad reaffirmed the adoption of non-cooperation in four stages; and appointed a committee with Gandhi as chairman to give practical effect to that policy. The Conference further decided to extend the Khilafat volunteer organizations all over India in order to collect funds and prepare the masses for non-cooperation. On 22 June, eighty-two Muslims submitted a memorial to the Viceroy, Reading, requesting him to impress upon the British government the vital necessity of revising the Turkish peace terms, and holding out the threat that, if their suggestions were not adopted, they would withdraw cooperation from the government with effect from

24 *Moslem Outlook*, 20 May 1920. For Mohamed Ali's criticism of the peace terms, see 'Denunciation of Peace Treaty', Iqbal (ed.), *Writings and Speeches*, pp. 195-204.

[illegible]

[illegible]
5th January 1921

Sir,

My son <u>Jahiruddin Ahmed</u> has returned from Aligarh and states that he has not been admitted into the College. The object of Gandhi ~~[illegible]~~ is simply to ruin the lives of Musalman students. I am afraid that he is succeeding in his object. My son assures me that he has <u>done</u> nothing to justifying the treatment he has received in your College. He never joined the Ali Brothers madmen's National University and never asked anyone to join that University. I hope at least Muhammadan college authorities will not help Gandhi & Co. in ruining the lives of Muhammadan students. I have not up to this time information what offence my son has committed for which his name has been struck off the College register, without calling upon him for an explanation or giving him an opportunity to disprove any complaints that might have been made against him.

In conclusion I beg to request that my son may be re-admitted into your College, and that if on for any special reasons which cannot be disclosed it is impossible to readmit him into your

college he may be given a
discharge certificate to
enable him to join some
other college.

As I have recd. no reply
from you to my previous
letters ~~say~~ on the subject
~~I send~~ this under a
registered cover to ensure
its reaching you.

Apologising for the trouble

given

Yours obediently
Ra Min Bukhsh
Sub Divl. Magistrate

My son was reading in the
second year class of your
college & occupied room No 38
in S.S. Court – RB

King Kothi,
Hyderabad-Deccan,
18th November 1920.

My dear Dr.Ziauddin Ahmad,

I enclose a letter in original which Abdullah Badshah, one of your senior students, has written me for transmission to you with my own recommendation for his pardon. My father and his grand-father were long partners of a well-known firm of Madras merchants. His father himself was my pupil in my pedagogic days. It was I who sent Abdullah Badshah to Aligarh many years ago and I have ever taken a great interest in his education. Knowing his quiet and docile nature, I never dreamt that he would ever bother himself with any political movement, much less a movement against his College authorities. I was under the impression he was among those students who were loyal to you. I was, therefore, greatly surprised and disappointed when I heard that he had joined Mr. Mohammad Ali and had even become his standard bearer. The news reached me rather late. I telegraphed to him my view. I am glad that he had the good sense to leave Aligarh and come here before Mr.Mohammad Ali was ejected from the College premises. Myself and my children have now converted him and brought him back to sanity. I believe he now sees his error. He says he joined the unfortunate movement only when he was misled into the belief that it was against the commands of the Quran to be in a Government-aided institution. I know he is an honest lad like his father.

He resembles his father very much both in appearance and character: (curiously enough, the father died the moment the son was born). He is now really sorry for all he did under a mistaken belief and begs you to pardon him. He has solemnly promised that he will have nothing to do with any political movement and specially with the non-co-operationists and that he will prove his sincerety by his obedience to you and his professors. May I, therefore, request you to be so kind as to pardon him and re-admit him nto the College ? If you again see him doing anything which you o not approve, kindly let me know and I shall see that he gives t up. I venture to think that I have some influence over him. e begs that you will kindly send him an admission card to enable im to join the College on the 1st December.

With kind regards,

Yours sincerely,

Ahmed Husain

(Aminjung)

1 August 1920. Gandhi sent a separate letter to the Viceroy, informing him that he was advising Muslims to adopt non-cooperation, because the peace terms violated ministerial pledges and disregarded Muslim sentiments. In justification of his decision, Gandhi wrote: 'I consider that a staunch Hindu wishing to live on terms of the closest friendship with my Mussalman countrymen, I should be an unworthy son of India if I did not stand by them in their hour of trial'.[25]

In September 1920, Gandhi presented his plan which called for a surrender of titles and honorary offices; refusal to attend levees and durbars; withdrawal from council elections; withdrawal of children from government schools and colleges; boycott of British courts by lawyers and litigants; refusal to serve in Mesopotamia; and boycott of foreign goods. After a prolonged debate this plan was approved by a vote of 148 to 133 in the Subjects Committee, and by 1,826 to 804 at the open session. At the Nagpur Congress in December where there were attempts to rescind the policy of non-cooperation, Gandhi once more emerged victorious. His resolution was ratified with only two dissentient voices. This was undoubtedly a great personal triumph for the Mahatma and a vindication of his political methods and strategy. The Chief Commissioner of the Central Provinces reported:

> The outstanding feature of the Congress has been the personal domination of Gandhi over all political leaders and followers alike. He has carried through the policy that he had decided for this Congress without any material modification . . . .The moderates of Nagpur were not heard; the extremist opponents under Khaparde and Moonje were brushed aside; Pandit Madan Mohan Malaviya's efforts were negatory; Jinnah carried no influence; Lajpat Rai wobbled and then became silent.[26]

V

Mohamed Ali and the Khilafat Delegation arrived in Bombay on 4 October 1920, at a time when the non-cooperation campaign was moving into its most active phase. At a meeting held to welcome

25 Gandhi to Chelmsford, 22 June 1920, *CWG*, vol. 17, p. 75.
26 F. Sly to Chelmsford, 1 January 1921, Chelmsford Papers (26).

his return to India he had only one piece of advice to offer to the Muslims: they must devote themselves whole-heartedly to the fight for Swaraj by plunging into the non-cooperation movement with their non-Muslim brethren, for only in this way would it be possible to achieve the Khilafat aims.[27]

Words were soon translated into deeds. Nine days after his return, he renewed his efforts to induce the Trustees of the M.A.O. College to give up the government grant-in-aid and to persuade students and teachers to leave the College at Aligarh and form the Jamia Millia Islamia (National Muslim University). While the trustees expressed their determination to run the institution on 'old established lines',[28] over 700 of the 1500 students answered Mohamed Ali's call. These included a group of devoted friends and followers who were to become prominent in later years—Zakir Husain, Mohammad Ashraf, S.M. Tonki, Abdul Hamid Khan, son of a judge in Dera Ismail Khan; Nurul Hasan of Azamgarh who was 'so impressed by the speeches of Azad and Azad Sobhani that I left College as a non-cooperator on the 27th October'[29] and Mohammad Abid Husain, an undergraduate student, who, on 24 October, wrote to Ziauddin, the Principal of the College:

> Respectfully I beg to inform you that I have got my doubts removed within the last four or five days, and I am now a strong supporter of non-cooperation . . .I can, and will read in your College only in case it is nationalised [sic]. Otherwise, I am ready to face the doom awating my non-cooperating brothers.[30]

The College authorities expelled the non-cooperators. But when this failed to check the growing spirit of non-cooperation, they decided to close down the College. The UP government went a

27 Watson, *op. cit.*, p. 63.

28 For a critical account of Mohamed Ali's activities in Aligarh during the non-cooperation movement, see Shaikh Mohammad Abdullah, *Mushahidat wa Ta'asurat* (Aligarh, 1969), pp. 294-5. For an appreciation of his role, see the essays in *Aligarh Magazine,* 1953-54 to 1954-55, *op. cit.* Of special interest are the articles of Abdul Ghaffar, K.M. Ashraf, Abdul Majid Daryabadi, and Ali Abbas Husaini.

29 A.M. Khan to Ziauddin, n.d. Papers relating to non-cooperation movement, Aligarh Muslim University Archives (AMUA).

30 M. Abid Husain to Ziauddin, 24 October 1920, *ibid.*

step further to stem the tide of non-cooperation; it suspended the scholarships of non-cooperating students, and dismissed many teachers in the neighbouring areas who were allegedly responsible for stirring trouble on the campus. Munshi Aziz Ahmad Zuberi, assistant master in the Government High School, Etah, was dismissed. Similarly, Bhu Deo Sharma, a teacher in the Anglo-Vernacular High School, Anupshahar, was considered 'an undesirable person for employment in recognised schools'. The government also sought the help of several Muslim landowners and the ruling chiefs to combat non-cooperation at Aligarh.[31]

By the end of 1920, the College authorities, in cooperation with the UP government, had cut off all the tall poppies at Aligarh, and the non-cooperation movement lost its vigour after the College was closed. After the closure of the College on 26 October, many students sought admission elsewhere, while others dissociated themselves from the agitation under paternal pressures, as the following letter indicates:

> My father has forced me to join your college once again, and I have reluctantly bowed to the parental authority. It is a mighty fall indeed. The whole enthusiasm ends in thin air. But you cannot realise under what great mental torture I am labouring today.[32]

The most determined, however, seceded from Aligarh and founded the Jamia Millia with the backing of Gandhi,[33] and with Mohamed

31 Hasan, *Nationalism and Communal Politics*, pp. 182-83.

32 M. Ibrahim Khan to Mirza, 15 November 1920, AMUA.

33 Gandhi campaigned actively for the Jamia Millia. On 24 October 1920 he urged the trustees of the Aligarh College to decline any further grant from the government, which was followed by an appeal to parents to withdraw their sons from the College. On 11 October, he visited Aligarh and spoke to the students on non-cooperation. In November, he returned to the city to participate in the Committee for framing a constitution for the National Muslim University. The meeting was held on 22 November. For the role of Gandhi, see *CWG*, vol. 18, pp. 221-22. 368-70; Home Poll. A, December 1920, 210-16, NAI.

For a vivid account of the drama which accompanied the establishment of Jamia Millia, see Abidullah Ghazi, 'Aligarh Tehrik awr Jamia Millia', *Aligarh Magazine*, *op. cit.*, pp. 263-276; Irshad-ul-Huq, 'Jamia Millia ki kahani', *A'aj Kal*, December 1978, pp. 30-34. An interesting note on the

Bombay,
Jan 31

Dear Mr. Ghate,

I was glad to receive your letter although it is a doleful one. I was wondering why I did not hear from you. My eye is fixed on Ali Brothers. I am simply waiting for the result of the Govt. inquiry. Nothing shd be done until the Report of that Committee [illegible]. Is the inquiry over? If as a result of the inquiry the Brothers are not released the time for action will have arrived. The responsibility for taking such action as will be necessary [illegible] on my shoulders and if I am at all well I shall not allow a single moment to pass in taking action and from the present state of my health I have every reason to hope that within a month

time I should be able to take [illegible]
work of the [illegible] [illegible]. My
medical adviser expects me to take fully
three months' rest outside India
after he discharges me. But for the
sake of this measure I should certainly
forego the three months' rest. I
agree with you that the new bill
for the preservation of internal tranquility
is dangerous and no stone may be
left unturned by us to kill the measure.
But I strongly feel that because of its
very severity it will never become law.
I think that all the Indian Members
of the Imperial Council will [illegible]
[illegible] it. But all this is no reason
for the Country not taking up [illegible]

agitation. I am myself preparing to
do my humble share in it. I am
watching its course. There is no fear
of its immediately becoming law. There
will therefore be ample time to discuss
and develop the strongest possible agitation.
In any event I would like the Sindhis
to keep rigorously clear of the agitation
until they have gained their first freedom.
I shall hope that they will take no
[illegible] [illegible] [illegible] with me

Yours Sincerely

M.K.Gandhi

Ali as its first Vice-Chancellor (*Sheikhul Jamia*). Though associated with the Jamia for many years, Mohamed Ali's enthusiasm for the institution was short-lived.[34] He devoted some time to giving the Jamia a solid Islamic footing, reviving Shibli's discourses on the Quran and making sure that 'our day began with a full hour devoted to the rapid exegesis of the Quran', but he was soon drawn into the vortex of politics.[35] In December 1920, Mohamed Ali resigned from his office, and headed, with a following of fifty students, for the Nagpur sessions of the Congress, the Muslim League, and the Khilafat Conference.

VI

There can be no doubt that Mohamed Ali was the preeminent leader amidst the perfervid activity of the Khilafat and non-cooperation campaigns. With his flowing beard and flowing gown, he exemplified self-confidence and bounce at the Khilafat meetings, influenced major policy decisions, and dictated the tone and content of various resolutions. He was among the busiest men in India, promoting the non-cooperation campaign by speaking before crowds and local committees and organising disciplined support for the programme. From January to February 1921, Mohamed Ali addressed meetings in several parts of eastern and western India. His presence at the Erode Session of the *Majlis-ul-ulama* in March gave a tremendous boost to the Khilafat movement, as did his presence in April, at various meetngs in Madras which attracted huge crowds of Hindus and Muslims. From April to August, Mohamed Ali spoke at conferences and meetings in various parts of UP: Meerut (9 April), Bulandshahr (12 April), Lucknow (1 May and 7 August), Moradabad (26 July and 6 August), Pilibhit and Sitapur (7 August), and Allahabad (10 August).[36] The whole of India was astir. The religious frenzy, generated by Mohamed Ali and other

Jamia Millia, inspired by the author's association with Zakir Husain, M. Mujeeb and Abid Husain, is by W.C. Smith, *Modern Islam in India* (Lahore, 1946).

34 This is the impression of, among others, Abdul Latif Azmi, assistant editor of *Jamia*, a monthly magazine in Urdu.

35 *My Life: A Fragment*, p. 29.

36 This is based on reports of his speeches in the records of the government of India. See Home Poll. 1921, 11, NAI; Home Poll. 1921-22, 194, NAI.

Khilafatists, swept the country in an unprecedented way. A popular song of the era reflected the spirit:

> So spoke the mother of Mohamed Ali
> My son, lay down your life for the sake of Khilafat

Mohamed Ali was also able to provide leadership to a newly-emerging secular leadership amongst Muslims, represented by Ansari, A.M. Khwaja, T.A.K. Sherwani, C. Khaliquzzaman, Shuaib Qureshi, Asaf Ali and A.R. Siddiqi. He was able to do so partly because of his skill in whipping up pan-Islamic passions, but mainly because of his close links with some influential western-educated Muslims and their allies amongst the *ulama*. These links were established during the Muslim University movement and strengthened through the *Anjuman-i-Khuddam-i-Ka'aba*. As a result, an impressive array of journalists, lawyers, doctors, university-men, and some Muslim divines—patronized and financed by the Raja of Mahmudabad and the Nawab of Bhopal—worked in close cooperation. But the prized trophy was no doubt Maulana Abdul Bari, the learned and renowned *alim*, whose influence extended far beyond the dark and narrow alleys of the Firangi Mahal in Lucknow.[37] Abdul Bari, noted more for his scholarship than for his political adroitness, played second-fiddle to Mohamed Ali during the Khilafat movement and lent his support to the *murids* fanciful projects, such as the ill-conceived *Hijrat* of 1920.[38]

37 A brief note on Mohamed Ali's association with Abdul Bari is in Mufti Reza Ansari, 'Maulana Mohamed Ali awr Maulana Firangi Mahali', *Jamia*, Jan-Feb., 1980.

38 There is no doubt that the idea of *Hijrat* was first conceived by Abul Kalam Azad who issued a *fatwa* accordingly. But Mohamed Ali was among the first Khilafat leaders who gave expression to the idea of *Hijrat* in a letter to the Viceroy. It is not known if his views on the issue were familiar to his colleagues. Mohamed Ali wrote:

> In view of our present weak condition, migration is the only alternative for us; and if we are forced either to forswear our faith or leave our Motherland, we could only migrate from this great country to which Islam brought its blessings more than twelve hundred years ago. A Mussalman is required by his faith, which is catholic and universal, to maintain an extraordinary detachment from country and race. But Islam is firmly based on the solid rock of human nature, and we are neither required to cultivate, nor have we in fact cultivated an unnatural

Mohamed Ali tried to influence Gandhi as well. But the Mahatma, who had humbled his more determined opponents both at Calcutta and Nagpur, was not to be outmanoeuvred. He not only determined the course of the Khilafat agitation, but also imposed his strict standards of discipline on the firebrand Ali Brothers.[39] Gandhi recognised his differences with the Ali Brothers, but cherished the hope that 'on seeing the success of my experiment in non-violence, (they) will come to realize its excellence and beauty later on'.[40] In May 1920, he conceded that all Muslims did not look at Non-cooperation 'from my angle', but referred to 'a distinct understanding with them that violence could never be allowed to go on side-by-side with non-violence'.[41]

Mohamed Ali was never shy of expressing his disagreement with the Gandhian techniques, particularly with his non-violent methods. Yet, he surrendered to Gandhi's leadership, expressed admiration for and placed his confidence in his techniques of mass mobilization. Speaking together with Gandhi at a mass meeting in Lucknow, Mohamed Ali declared that Indian Muslims 'have chosen the

indifference to the land we live in, or to the good people who inhabit it along with us. Millions of ties that have been formed in our twelve-century long sojourn in India would seek to keep us tied down to it; and when we migrate as we must, the minarets of our mosques would continue to beckon to us, and their domes, that would resound no more wtih the cries of 'God is Greatest', would by their very silence recall us to them. And even if we proved unresponsive to the fraternal calls of the living, the non-Muslim compatriots with whom we have for so many centuries wrought for the good of our Motherland, and have together developed India's marvellous Arts and culture, graves of our ancestors would exercise over us their spiritual spell. But a greater call would make us leave this dear land of ours—never dearer than now that we would be taking our leave of it—for it would be the imperative call of religious duty. Mohamed Ali to Chelmsford, 24 April 1919, MAP.

39 The success of this was noticed by, among others, C.Y. Chintamani. 'I had seen the latter (Mohamed Ali) more than a decade ago. How completely he has been transformed. Great I believe has been the Gandhian influence over him', he wrote. Chintamani to Srinivasa Sastri, 6 October 1924, T.N. Jagadisan (ed.), *Letters of V.S. Srinivasa Sastri* (Asia Publishing House, 1963 edn), pp. 139-40.

40 See Brown, *Gandhi's Rise to Power*, p. 331, f.n.2.

41 *Day-to-Day*, vol. 2, p. 238.

path of non-violent non-cooperation in the belief that by this course they could best secure the interests of their country and their faith'.[42] He reaffirmed in December 1923 that 'our compact is that as long as I am associated with him I shall not resort to the use of force even for purposes of self-defence.[43] From Paris, where Mohamed Ali had gone as member of the Khilafat Delegation, he wrote: 'I only wish that I had a Musheer here, and if possible Fazlul Haq, though of course the best man to have is Gandhiji himself'.[44] He was also accused of being a Gandhiphile, but his reply was :

> I cannot find in any community—Jewish, Christian or any other a man who has as noble a character as Mahatma Gandhi. My *pir* and *murshid* is Abdul Bari whom I greatly respect. Yet I can say that I have not found any one superior to Mahatma Gandhi.[45]

There can be no doubt that such sentiments for 'our guide, philosopher and friend' were genuinely inspired. But it is equally important to remember that the Khilafatists, in general, were anxious to placate the Mahatma (who tolerated no dissent) in order to sustain his enthusiasm for the Khilafat cause. Subservience to Gandhi was 'distasteful', particularly from the point of view of some orthodox *ulama*, but was imperative in order to ensure his participation in the Khilafat movement. This view was best summed up by Mohamed Ali in July 1921. He said :

> . . . . . .when the Congress was adopting for the first time the Khilafat programme of non-violent non-cooperation, the essential thing was the unity of Hindus and Muslims and even if Muslims had been ready for violence, which they were not, they could'nt have succeeded without Hindu goodwill——Long before we were free we had made up our minds to bring about a complete *entente* between Hindus and Muslims. . . .and the

42 This and other references on the subject are in Brown, *Gandhi's Rise to Power*; Robinson, *Separatism Among Muslims*, also, Bamford, *Histories*, p, 166.

43 *Ibid.*

44 Mohamed Ali to Shaukat Ali, 15 May 1920, MAP.

45 Mohamed Ali to Swami Shraddhanand, 26 March 1924, *ibid.*

> best man among the Hindus to deal with was Mahatma Gandhi, a peace-loving and non-violent patriot who was intensely religious without a fury of a theologian and whose honesty all could rely upon. He found us to be equally religious and equally without the fury of the theologian, and as Muslims we could not pledge ourselves to remain non-violent in all circumstances, he found that we too regarded force at present to be futile, and above all he could trust our word as much as we trusted him. Even if we ourselves wished to use force immediately, which we did not and could not, we would have lost his support and thus have lost the chance of bringing about the Hindu-Muslim *entente* and of bringing the government to its senses.[46]

While Mohamed Ali was reaffirming his loyalty to Gandhi, the Khilafat Conference at Karachi (of which he was the President), passed a resolution that it was *haram* for Muslims to serve in the army or police force. Two months later he was arrested. On 26 October 1922 began the trial where he made the famous statement: 'The trial is not "Mohamed Ali and six others *versus* the Crown", but "God *versus* man". The case is therefore between God and man. The whole question is "Shall God dominate over man or shall man dominate over God ?"[47] The jury was not impressed. On 1 November Mohamed Ali and five Muslim leaders were sentenced to two years' rigorous imprisonment.

46 Brown, *Gandhi's Rise to Power*, pp. 330-31.
47 'Gentlemen of the Jury', in Iqbal (ed.), *Writings and Speeches*, pp. 205-44.

4

MOHAMED ALI AND THE CONGRESS: DEVOTION AND DISILLUSIONMENT

During Mohamed Ali's imprisonment—1 November 1922 to 28 August 1923—there were dramatic changes in the state of affairs in the country. One of the notable changes was that the edifice of communal unity crumbled and mutual recriminations between the Khilafatists and their Hindu allies inspired some of the communal disturbances in various parts of the country. Many of the champions of Hindu-Muslim unity executed a *volte face* and thought it fit to swim with the current of communalism, to revitalise it, and to perpetuate it, if possible. Communal antipathies also sharpened following disputes over cow-slaughter and the playing of music before mosques. From March to July 1923, there were riots in Amritsar, Multan, Moradabad, Meerut, and Allahabad. In August and September there were further outbreaks at Amritsar, Panipat, Gonda, Jabalpur, Agra, Saharanpur and Rae Bareli. In 1924, the frequency of riots increased. From April to October, there were violent clashes in Hapur, Delhi, Lahore, Lucknow, Moradabad, Bhagalpur, Shahjahanpur, Allahabad, and Kohat.

These developments seem to suggest that the assumption on which Gandhi sought to unite Hindus and Muslims during the Khilafat and Non-cooperation movements was untenable. He, no doubt succeeded in uniting a number of incompatible, even antagonistic, elements in a seemingly common political struggle. Caught up in their millennium-seeking exhiliration, the leaders 'lived in a kind of intoxication during the year 1921—full of excitement and optimism and a bouyant enthusiasm'. But every further step in the progress of non-cooperation tended to split them up into separate factions. Thus we find the early communist movement correctly putting forward its idea of forging Hindu-Muslim unity on the basis of the unity of the exploited masses in the anti-imperialist struggle and criticising the weakness of Hindu-Muslim unity in the Khilafat agitation. The root cause of the communal troubles, stated its 'Manifesto on the Hindu-Moslem unity and Swaraj' was that:

> religion was allowed to play the chief part in the movement. It may be comparatively easy to fire politically backward people with religious fanaticism; but it is impossible, even dangerous, to base a political movement on such unreliable grounds. The recent occurrences amply prove this impossibility and dangerousness. If the hostility against British imperialism is made a religious issue, the hostility thus aroused can at any moment turn into antagonism among the two great Indian communities as they do not profess the same religion. It is precisely what happened now.[1]

The Khilafat demands, noted the manifesto:

> constituted one of the principal planks of the non-cooperation platform. The Khilafat movement however was essentially a political movement based on religious principles. The Ali Brothers and other Moslem leaders succeeded in convincing the Mahatma that the Khilafat problem was to Indian Moslems a question of life and death. The Mahatma being himself a religious man assumed the championship of the Khilafat movement, and a bargain was struck—Hindus to support the Khilafat agitation and Moslems to take active part in Swaraj movement and perhaps by and by give up cow-killing and spare the religious sentiments of their Hindu countrymen. This was the basis of the union. *It was artificial in that it did not take into account operation of the material forces which alone could bring about a solid and durable unity. It was built on the unreliable foundation of religious sentimentalism* (emphasis added).

1 G. Adhikari (ed.), *Documents of the History of the Communist Party of India, 1923-1925* (Delhi, 1974), vol. 2, p. 210.

The present debacle was a foregone conclusion of such an ill-started movement.[2]

The growth of inter-communal antagonism, referred to in the manifesto, was the consequence of several complex factors: the Moplah riots of August 1921 which led to the killing of Hindus and Muslims, 'with the ardour of an oppressed class rising against its enemies, the ardour of religious fanaticism destroying sin and establishing a kingdom of good';[3] the revival of *shuddhi*, *sangathan*, *tabligh* and *tanzim* movements as the outcome of the introduction of religion into politics and the overall heightening of communal consciousness; and the introduction of Montagu-Chelmsford Reforms which led to an intense struggle for power, influence and status in the newly-created 'self-governing' bodies.[4] No less important was the impact of Gandhi's decision to suspend civil disobedience in March 1922, a decision which not only demoralised the leaders but also created frustration among the masses. The bottled-up energy of the people, unleashed during the non-cooperation days, now found an outlet in communal clashes. The Non-cooperation movement, wrote a leading Communist commentator, 'has been brought to a close. No sophistry, no loud talk to the gallery, which is being done amply, can change the fact. . . .The programme of organising a countrywide mass movement with the purpose of challenging the authority of the British government has been abandoned'.[5] Hindu-Muslim unity of the non-cooperation days, which rested on 'chimeral metaphysics' only, was a thing of

2 *Ibid.*, p. 211.

3 Smith, *Modern Islam in India*, p. 203.

4 For details, see Mushirul Hasan, Communalism in the Provinces: A case Study of Bengal and the Punjab, 1922-1926, *Economic and Political Weekly*, 16 August 1980.

5 M.N. Roy, September 1923, in *Adhikari* (*ed.*), *Documents*, p. 178. According to Roy, the 'philosophy of non-cooperation was fed with the cult of inspiration. It was hero-worship. It sunk so deeply in the morass of this deplorable subjectivism that the vision of the forces impelling it was altogether lost. The leaders of non-cooperation believed that they could lead the movement, not according to the dictates of the objective forces that gave it birth, but to suit their own desires. In short, the leaders conspired against the very forces that had created them'. M.N. Roy, April 1923, *ibid.*, p. 174.

the past. Wrote the *Socialist*, an organ of the Communist movement in India, in March 1923:

> The Hindu-Muslim unity was boomed outright in flamboyant headings in newspapers and big leaders, Hindu and Mohamedan, embraced each other on public platforms or dined in common plates, at the common table in restaurant cars when on tour. But mass-Hindu and mass-Mahomedan knew nothing about these *lilas* of the upper gods on the high spiritual plane. They only saw the beautiful pantomimes and cheered lustily perhaps; and soon forgot everything about it. It was inevitable. And now all the newspaper boom has vanished and the tocsin is rung that the Hindu-Muslim unity is in grave danger in the Punjab. It is easy to find once or twice the cause of all this in our enemy's gold or diplomacy but that doesn't help always.[6]

Gandhi's decision to suspend civil disobedience took the sting out of the Muslim agitation. The Khilafatists were disappointed and angry. At the meetings of the *Jamiyat-i-Ulama* and the Central Khilafat Committee in March 1922, Gandhi was condemned for his 'betrayal'. Hasrat Mohani rejected the Bardoli programme on the ground that, if religion enjoined violence, a policy of non-violence could not be adopted. At the *Jamiyat-i-Ulama* Conference held in Ajmer, Abdul Bari created a consternation by attacking the Mahatma and the Bardoli resolution, adopted by the Congress Working Committee. Such attacks continued after Gandhi's arrest on 10 March 1922. The Muslims were left to stew in their own juice. They felt betrayed and abandoned. When Gandhi returned from prison in February 1924, his interest—whatever little was left—in the Khilafat had evaporated. When asked to nominate a Hindu to join a Khilafat deputation to Angora, the Mahatma declined on the grounds that it would be 'out of place' for any Hindu to do so. How ironical that five years earlier he had urged his co-religionists to support the 'just cause of the Muslims', and said: 'for the Hindus not to support them [Muslims] to the utmost would be a cowardly breach of brotherhood'.[7]

6 *Adhikari (ed.), Documents*, p. 199.
7 Hasan, *Nationalism and Communal Politics*, pp. 193-94.

After the suspension of civil disobedience, Muslims had yet another surprise in store. On 21 November 1922, the Turkish National Assembly at Ankara decided to separate the Khilafat from the Sultanate. And since the maintenance of the temporal power of the Khalifa was one of the main objects of the Khilafat movement, this action by a purely Muslim body completely took the wind out of its sails. In March 1924, the final blow was struck by Mustafa Kamal Pasha who burst the bubble of the Khilafat. Its immediate result was the disruption of the Khilafat Party. From 1918 to 1922, both religious zeal and the over-whelming anti-colonial sentiment united various Muslim groups. But once the initial Khilafat euphoria had worn thin, the inherent contradictions in the alliance destroyed the facade of unity and brought to surface the division among the ranks of the *ulama*, as among the Muslims in general. The *Jamiyat-i-Ulama* was divided with Nisar Ahmad of Kanpur and Abdul Majid of Budaun joining the *tanzim* movement; they also founded a parallel organization of *Jamiyat-i-Ulama-i-Hind* in Kanpur.[8] Abdul Bari, the erstwhile apostle of Hindu-Muslim unity, spoke the language of a zealot, urging Muslims to sacrifice cows without regard for Hindu feelings.[9]

This is not all. The rapprochement between the political and religious wings of the Khilafat movement was unable to sustain itself in part because international developments had undermined its *raison d'etre*, and, in part, because there was no sound basis for permanent adjustments of diversified and, in some cases, conflicting interests.[10] Leaders like Hakim Ajmal Khan, Khaliquzzaman, T.A.K. Sherwani and Syed Zahur Ahmad joined the Congress-Khilafat-Swaraj Party after the defeat of the 'pro-changers' at the Gaya Congress in 1923, leaving the *ulama* to continue their lone battle against council entry. During 1923, the Swarajist band-wagon gathered way amidst a flurry of attempts at compromise with those opposed to entering the councils. By May 1923, the All-India Congress Committee had decided to cease its propaganda against council entry, and, by August, the Swarajists felt strong enough to ignore the All-India Congress Committee and attack the

8 I.H. Qureshi, *Ulema in Politics: A study relating to the political activities of the ulema in the South-Asian Subcontinent* (Karachi, 1974 edn.), p. 302.

9 See Robinson, *Separatism Among Indian Muslims*, p. 339.

10 Faruqi, *The Deoband School*, p. 67.

ulama.[11] The *ulama* were totally dismayed. They slept upon their illusive victory at Gaya and woke up to see the Khilafat leadership out of their hands. All they could do was to hurl vituperation upon their erstwhile allies. 'Those who pretended to be our friends at one time and made a catspaw of the ulama now seem anxious to get rid of them', complained Abdul Bari.[12]

One of the immediate consequences of such developments was the disappearance of the Muslim divines from the national scene. They had no doubt gained in confidence and self-consciousness from the time of the Muslim League session in 1918, but the set-back to the Khilafat cause shattered their plans and brought to an end their growing influence in national politics. The result was: bewilderment, confusion, and even inactivity. Having once mobilised new groups, roused their religious fervour, and articulated their grievances, the *ulama* were now like a contrary jack-in-box refuring to retire, to seek now outlets for their energy, and to build something positive out of the Khilafat experience. Some doggedly kept the Khilafat movement gasping, some capitulated to the communalist camp, but most, including the *ulama* of Deoband, entered the arena of religious controversies and organized the *tabligh* and *tanzim* societies as a counterpart to *shuddhi* and *sangthan*.

The Khilafat agitation provided the *ulama* with distinct enemy and goals; when the enemy and goals proved elusive other whipping boys and solutions had to be found. Much of their interests, geared to religious goals, remained, because they seemed to be the hope for the Muslim community. In consequence, many of the *ulama* who participated in the Khilafat movement reverted to their former religious preoccupations. The *Jamiyat-i-Ulama*, despite its nationalist sympathies, moved along a course parallel to that of the nationalist Muslim political leadership. It was mainly concerned to secure safeguards against interference with the *sharia* and guarantees for its propagation and implementation. In 1940, however, a section of the *Jamiyat* became the nucleus of various nationalist organizations. The Congress, which was otherwise vociferous about the secularization of politics, was ever ready to

11 Robinson, *Separatism Among Indian Muslims*, pp. 339-341.

12 Statement to the Press, 20 August 1923, Abdul Bari Papers, Firangi Mahal, Lucknow.

exploit this reserve of influence to counteract the Muslim League.[13]

The *ulama* of Firangi Mahal also failed to adapt themselves to the changing realities of Indian politics and were unable to provide leadership to the Muslim community. Abdul Bari, the chief architect of the alliance between the *ulama* and the Congress, became increasingly despondent, isolated, and alienated from the Congress. In August 1923, he complained:

> The position of the Muslims has been rendered very awkward. Those who pretended to be our friends at one time and made a catspaw of the *ulama* now seem anxious to get rid of them.[14]

Abdul Bari was right. The *ulama* had been brought into political life because of their influence in the countryside and their ability to gather various groups under their own banner. But in the aftermath of civil disobedience and the Khilafat fiasco, the issues which concerned Indian leaders were of a political nature; so the services of the *ulama* were no longer required. They were bluntly told not to dabble in politics. In a public meeting at Lucknow in August 1923, Motilal Nehru regretted that the Muslims had given 'so much latitude' to the *ulama* and argued that 'they should insist in future that the ulemas [sic] refrain from meddling in politics'.[15]

II

Mohamed Ali was released from prison on 29 August 1923, and in his first public address spoke of his gloom at finding on his shoulders the burden of freeing Islam and India. Non-cooperation was still the main plank of his politics as reflected in his statement: 'If cooperation was "haram" according the the Islamic law two years ago, it cannot become "halal" today'.[16] At the same time,

13 For a brief outline of the role of the *ulama*, see Mushirul Hasan, 'Religion and Politics: The Ulama and the Khilafat Movement', *Economic and Political Weekly*, 15 May 1981.

14 See f.n. 12 above.

15 *Leader*, 3 January 1922, quoted in Robinson, *Separatism Among Indian Muslims*, p. 340.

16 *Ibid.*, f.n. 6, p. 340. In September 1923, he complained that the Swarajists have 'completely gone back on the entire creed and policy of Gandhi'. 'I have been realizing every day that the leaders of the Swaraj Party want

he criticised the Swaraj Party and its leader, Motilal Nehru, for starting chamber practice which could not be reconciled with the Congress decision to boycott British law courts.[17] But three weeks later, it was Mohamed Ali who proposed the compromise resolution at the Delhi Special Congress, permitting 'such Congressmen as have no religious or other conscientious objections against entering the legislatures. . .to stand as candidates', and calling for 'united endeavours to achieve Swaraj at the earliest moment'. The reason for this sudden change of mind was probably the one which influenced Jawaharlal Nehru as well: the absence of any political programme before the country and the failure of 'no-changers' to satisfy those who believed in parliamentary activity after an important phase of direct political action.[18] It is also possible to argue that Mohamed Ali's decision was motivated by the desire to resolve the differences between various Congress groups and to unite the warring factions. Such a desire was most explicitly expressed in a letter to Jawaharlal Nehru who was induced to accept, much against his will, the Congress Secretaryship in Mohamed Ali's year of presidentship.[19] In an impressive appeal for unity, Mohamed Ali wrote:

> Let the Provincial Congress [UP] assembly send for the sacred soil of Kashi itself the message of the greater and more solid *sangathan*, the *sangathan* of the National Congress. And let us go forth from this Conference truly *shuddh*, purged of all narrowness, bigotry and intolerance in order to free our country from the most cramping slavery—the slavery not only of the body but also of the soul. . . If there is anything of the old world spirituality in Kashi, let us recommence the work of our

to throw Gandhism overboard without some of them having the courage to confess it', he wrote to his Khilafat comrade, Saifuddin Kitchlew. He wanted Kitchlew to play the role of peacemaker between him and the 'Gujrati friends', though he advised 'caution and restraint'. Mohamed Ali to Kitchlew, 30 September 1923, Hailey Papers, MSS. EUR. 220 (7-A), IOL.

17 Jafri, *Sirat*, pp. 350-2.

18 Nehru, *An Autobiography*, p. 99.

19 *Ibid.*, p. 117.

great chief, Gandhiji, in the spirit of religious devotion and utter unworldiness.[20]

Whatever the motives, Mohamed Ali's decision to go along with the Swarajists disappointed his friends, colleagues and admirers. The *ulama*, in particular, were enraged because their council entry *fatwa* was ignored : the once powerful voice of theocracy was thus drowned in the passionate appeals for unity.[21] So were the 'no-changers' who accused their idol of having betrayed the heritage of the Mahatma.[22] M.N. Roy, a leading member of the Communist movement in India, summed up the resentment towards Mohamed Ali's *volte face* in the *Aftermath of Non-cooperation*, published in 1926.

> Much was expected of Mohamed Ali. The rank and file of the Congress, which revolted against the revolt of radicalism, heroically held its own until the second in command of the non-cooperation movement came out of jail, in order to rally the scattered forces for new action. The hope has been dashed to the ground. The idol showed its clay feet in such a hurry that the admirers were staggered. Mohamed Ali has failed to give the leadership which was expected of him. His pronouncements since he came out of jail are full of mere platitudes and hopeless contradictions. No constructive programme, no positive suggestion as to the future of the movement is to be found in them. He authorises the removal of the ban on the councils, but holds up the edict of the ulemas [*sic*] on the question. He professes to be the standard-bearer of pure Gandhism, but sets his face positively against civil disobedience, without which the political programme of non-cooperation becomes meaningless. He indulges in fearful threats against the government, but finds the demand for the separation from the British empire 'childish and petulant'. He deplores the Hindu-Moslem feuds, but still insists on khilafat propaganda,

20 Mohamed Ali to Jawaharlal Nehru, n.d., 1923, in J. Nehru (ed.), *A Bunch of Old Letters* (Bombay, 1966 edn.), pp. 30-1.

21 *Leader*, 20 September 1923, quoted in Robinson, *Separatism Among Indian Muslims*, p. 341.

22 Adhikari (ed.), *Documents*, p. 181.

which contributed not a little to the success of the enemies of national freedom in creating communal dissensions, and incidentally to the organisation of the forces of Hindu reaction in the Hindu Sabha, which is sure to aggravate the communal issues. In political questions, he has absolutely no programme to suggest. He harps on the threadbare 'constructive programme' which constructs naught but inaction. Such is the record with which Mohamed Ali goes to Cocanada to furnish the nationalist forces with a new direction.[23]

In December 1923, Mohamed Ali delivered his Presidential Address at the Kakinada Congress. Though described in a section of the press as the 'story of the Islamic faddist from sectarianism to nationalism',[24] the address provided a fuller explication of Mohamed Ali's ideas about Indian politics and the Muslim part therein. It therefore deserves serious consideration.[25]

Mohamed Ali reviewed thoroughly the past half-century in terms of nationalism and Hindu-Muslim unity. The main tenor was that unity had grown no less essential during the past few years, but still absolutely necessary if Indians hoped to realize their aims. Similarly, non-cooperation was not outmoded; even if one were to grant (only for the sake of argument) that non-cooperation had failed, there was no alternative to that programme.[26] 'You have no alternative better than Non-cooperation with the foreigner and cooperation with our neighbours', he said. All India must therefore follow the course to which they had pledged themselves.[27]

Mohamed Ali spoke of his long-standing dream of a 'Federation of Faiths', a 'United Faiths of India'.[28] India's millions, he said,

23 *Adhikari (ed.), Documents*, pp. 223-24.

24 *Bengalee*, 29 December 1912. Mohamed Ali's address, according to an intelligence report, 'has not been well received by the Hindus. . . Some of the prominent Hindus sitting around me near the dias said that the address was unsuggestive and prolix; others said that it was more Muslim history, and a tale of loyalty unrewarded and disregarded than an address of the President of the Congress'. Report by Tassaduk Husain, 31 December 1923, Foreign and Poll. Dept., 226(3)-X, External, NAI.

25 The summary of the Presidential Address is mainly based on Watson' *op. cit.*

26 Iqbal (ed.), *Writings and Speeches*, p. 285.

27 *Ibid.*, p. 286.

28 *Ibid.*, p. 256.

were so divided into communities and sects that Providence has created for us the mission of solving a unique problem and working out a new synthesis, which was nothing less than a Federation of Faiths'.[29] The synthesis, he argued, must be of a federal type, for the lines of cleavage were too deep to allow for any other sort of union. He went on to add:

> For more than twenty years I have dreamed the dream of a federation, grander, nobler and infinitely more spiritual than the United States of America, and today when many a political Cassandra prophesies a return to the bad old days of Hindu-Muslim dissensions, I still dream of 'United Faiths of India'. It was in order to translate this dream into reality that I had launched my weekly newspaper, and had significantly called it *The Comrade*—"Comrade of all and partisan of none".[30]

Mohamed Ali also dealt with the communal problem in a 'dispassionate' and ,impartial' manner,[31] suggesting various measurers to reduce communal antagonism and pleading for understanding, tolerance, for renewed vigour and determination. He regarded the Lucknow Pact arrangement of communal representation satisfactory for the time being, but added that Indians should hasten the pace to Swaraj 'so that we may readjust communal shares in representative bodies'.

The motives for Indian Muslim efforts towards Swaraj were still dual, according to Mohamed Ali. They aimed at freeing India and freeing Islam. The relationship between Indians and the Turks was in the nature of a compact, because both Turkey and India were oppressed by the same imperialism. Once India was free and her forces could not be driven to fight against the Turks, both Turkey and Islam would be safe. On the other hand, it was in order to keep India enslaved that Britain insisted on such harsh terms for the Ottoman Empire. Presumably he meant, as John Watson has suggested, that the Turks would have fought for the freedom of their co-religionists, including the Indian Muslims, and hence India, if they had not been so weakened. If so, his lack of

29 *Iqbal (ed.), Writings and Speeches*, p. 256.

30 *Ibid.*

31 *Amrita Bazar Patrika*, 29 December 1923.

realism in assessing the aims of the Turks did not stop here.[32] Although the Kamalist Revolution was on its way to achieving success and glory, Mohamed Ali still pictured them as fighting for the ideal Khalifa:

> I feel confident that once they are free from the distractions inevitable after the victories both of war and peace they will revive with God's assistance the glories not of Omayyad or Abbasid Empires, but of the first thirty years of the Khilafat before there were any kings or dynasties.[33]

He added that he had his own views on 'the possible adjustment of the relations of all Muslim states and the Khalifa', but that this was not the time to state them.

It is clear from the above summary that Mohamed Ali's Presidential Address was, in some respects, a faithful exposition of Indian nationalism, though the pan-Islamic strain in his thinking caused uneasiness in Congress circles. His survey of Hindu-Muslim relations, his assesment of the Congress movement, and his understanding of British imperialism was both perceptive and convincing. In fact it is striking to note his continued devotion to the Congress movement, as indeed to its leader, Gandhi, 'the most Christ-like man of our times'.[34] 'It is Gandhi, Gandhi, Gandhi, that has got to be dinned into the people's ears', he wrote to Saifuddin Kitchlew, 'because he means Hindu-Muslim unity, non-cooperation, *Swadharma* and *Swaraja*, while the rest are after petty communal or local ideals, most of them tinged with personal ambitions'.[35]

While Mohamed Ali was exhorting his audience to forge unity, Hindus and Muslims were engaged in a bitter feud leading to a steady deterioration of communal relations. In 1924, the frequency of riots increased in many parts of the country, the most serious being the one at Kohat in the North-West Frontier Province. It was against this background that Gandhi declared, on 18 September 1924, that he would fast for three weeks. Again, it was over the Kohat riots that, for the first time, differences between Gandhi and

32 Watson, *op. cit.*, p. 73.
33 Quoted in *ibid.*
34 Iqbal (ed.), *Writings and Speeches*, p. 276.
35 Quoted in Iqbal, *Life and Times*, p. 308.

the Muslim leaders, particularly Mohamed Ali, were revealed. The wheel had turned full circle. Within months of his exhortation at the Congress session in December 1923, Mohamed Ali gradually drifted away from the Congress, or, perhaps, as he would have put it, the Congress drifted away from him. The rift widened, estrangement grew.

III

By the end of 1924, Mohamed Ali's enthusiasm for the Congress seemed to dampen. This had a great deal to do with worsening Hindu-Muslim relations, reflected in the eruption of communal violence, in the resurgence of *tabligh*, *tanzim*, *shuddhi* and *sangathan* movements, and in the growth of communal alignments in the various 'self-governing' bodies. The Congres—once the rallying point for influential Muslim groups—was gradually loosing their support and, in the perception of some of its former allies, fostering communalism with a view to establishing 'Hindu Raj'. The Muslim League, relegated into the background during the Khilafat movement, was resucitated and gained a fresh lease of life in the midst of increasing communal strife. These were signs of widening Hindu-Muslim chasm in Indian politics.

Given the nature of the communal problem, individual efforts to ease tension and to resolve sources of friction could hardly prove rewarding; hence the failure of Gandhian initiatives in the form of fasts, unity conferences, and mutual pacts. 'Boards of arbitration, peace syndicates and solemn pacts about cows', Mohamed Ali wrote in early 1912, 'cannot solve it [communal problem] any more than we can by a spell of occult words control the winds and the tides'.[36] After 1924, in particular, such symbolic expressions were of no avail. In fact, it seemed superfluous for leaders of various communities to demonstrate their own concord. Communalism, which had struck deeper roots in society, could only be undermined through a massive social and economic transformation—a process which, according to some Congress stalwarts, had to be initiated after independence. This was stated by Gandhi in his corres-

36 Iqbal (ed.), *Writings and Speeches*, p. 70.

pondence with Ansari in early 1930,[37] and, more explicitly, by Motilal Nehru. In February 1930, he conceded:

> Both you and I have for years past been working as hard as we could to lay a solid foundation for this unity. But it has to be confessed that we have failed miserably. As a result of past experience and anxious thought I have now reached the conclusion that the lines upon which we worked were fundamentally wrong. . .The fact is that we have been appealing to the wrong court all these years. We may go on doing so to the end of eternity but will get no relief . . .It is now my firm conviction that Hindu-Muslim unity cannot be achieved by preaching it. We have to bring it about in a manner which will accomplish it without either Hindus or Muslims realising that they are working for unity. This can only be done on an economic basis and in the course of the fight for freedom from the usurper. When one community is fighting for the right to live which is common to both it is impossible to conceive that the other community will not sooner or later realise the consequences of success or failure. And having realised those consequences it is equally impossible to conceive that it will not throw itself wholeheartedly into the conflict. The mastermind has amidst much ridicule and misrepresentation discovered one such economic basis in the breaking of the salt law. The thing, to use his own favourite phrase, is 'incredibly simple'. The only wonder is that no one else ever thought of it. It is impossible to say at this stage whether even so simple a thing will catch the imagination of the people but if it does a tremendous victory is assured to both Hindus and Muslims. If it does not there is no hope for us and it is idle to talk of Hindu-Muslim unity and constitutional and communal rights.[38]

The Nationalist Muslims, who generally shared Congress' perception of the communal issues, continued to pin their hopes in a mutually acceptable constitutional concordat; so they often acted as mediators between the Congress and Muslim League leadership.

37 Gandhi to Ansari, 16 February 1930, in Hasan (ed.), *Muslims and the Congress*, pp. 101-102.

38 Motilal Nehru to Ansari, 17 February 1930, *ibid.*, p. 103.

The Nationalist Muslim Party, founded in July 1929 by Ansari and Azad, performed such a role. But its activities were greatly hampered because of its image which was indissolubly linked with the Congress, lending credence to the charge that Nationalist Muslims were subservient to the 'Hindu Mahasabha dominated Congress'. Shaukat Ali echoed such sentiments in April 1929, accusing Nationalist Muslims of being 'weak men and renegades, and, yielding to the open threats of Hindus, (to) have chosen to live at their mercy'.[39] He was particularly bitter with Ansari, president of the All-Parties National Convention held in December 1928, chiding him for playing the 'generous liberal minded patriot at the expense of one's people',[40] and for his 'adherence to Motilal Nehru and other Hindus'.[41] He described the Congress as 'an adjunct of the Hindu Mahasabha' and assailed its leadership for rejecting the Delhi Proposals after having accepted them at the Madras Congress in December 1927. 'It is you who has changed',

39 Shaukat Ali to Syed Mahmud, 26 April 1929, V.N. Datta and B.E. Cleghorn (eds.), *A Nationalist Muslim and Indian Politics: Being the Selected Correspondence of the late Dr. Syed Mahmud* (Delhi, 1974), p. 94. Shaukat Ali wrote in a similar vein about the Congress leaders:

> I have a complaint against Motilal and our Hindu co-workers, including Mahatma Gandhi, that they have got the Muslims fragmented but have themselves united. Now they are carrying on negotiations at high Govt. level to suppress the voice of the Muslims. I was opposed to Motilal. It was meaningless to fight us by enlisting the support of Ansari and other of my friends. You have said that your group has greatly changed. Our opinions, intentions, thoughts and principles have not suffered any change. I am a great opponent today of British rule and the Muslims are ready for every sacrifice for liberation. We shall now restrain the Muslims from any more sycophancy. But I feel upset because of the infidelity of Hindu friends and their hatred and contempt of the Muslims. Until they come to us with a clean mind and reach an honourable understanding with us, we shall not work with them. We will not be to blame if they work separately and suffer humiliation and we work separately unsuccessfully. When they come to us with a clean mind, we shall unite with them. This is the proper way to set their thinking on right lines. But if they decide to fight us, we shall give them a fight which they will long remember. You are pessimistic about the Muslims, but I am not. A Muslim is a good friend but a valiant foe. He can be cheated only once.

40 Shaukat Ali to Ansari, 6 September 1929, AICC Papers (105), NML.

Shaukat Ali to Ansari, 19 May 1929, Hasan (ed.), *Muslims and the Congress*, p. 70.

he wrote to Ansari, 'while the Central Khilafat Committee and I stand where we were, not in a spirit of obstinacy because we consider Motilal and his committee [Nehru Committee] have intentionally treated the Muslim point of view with undeserved contempt'.[42] Again,

> I know the present Hindu mentality well. They do not want our friendship; they want our allegiance and God willing, they will never get that. For any honourable peace and pact we are always ready but not for the slavery of the Hindus; just as we do not want to remain slaves of the English . . .Non-cooperation was ruined by these [Hindus] people, chances for Hindu-Muslim friendship throttled, an understanding between princes and people thwarted, the Swaraj Party dismembered and now you yourself see what is being done to kill the Congress, which has ceased to be National now. It has become an adjunct of the Hindu Mahasabha and will soon be a seeker of favours at the door of the British. The Muslims trust in God and would stand on their own legs.[33]

Mohamed Ali shared this view of the Congress because he had developed a point of view from which everything said or done by any Hindu or Nationalist Muslim appeared to be the direct result of Hindu Mahasabha influence. He exaggerated the influence of Hindu Mahasabha and failed to rcognise the importance of the secular elements in Congress which vigorously opposed communalism. His 'new mentality', as Ansari noted, 'admits of only two divisions in India, Hindu and Muslim, and not Nationalist and reactionary or non-cooperating'.[44] This was the limited framework of his analysis, though it was supposedly evolved in reaction to the growing ascendancy of communal and revivalist elements in the Congress. Mohamed Ali's feelings towards such elements were strong and mixed, and for some time past his hostile feelings towards Madan Mohan Malaviya and Lala Lajpat Rai had been predominant.[45] His long standing grievance was that the Congress,

42 Shaukat Ali to Ansari, 6 September 1929, AICC Papers (105).

43 Shaukat Ali to Ansari, 19 May 1929, Hasan (ed.), *op. cit.*

44 Ansari to Mazharul Haq, 7 September 1929, *ibid.*, pp. 86-87.

45 Mohamed Ali to Jawaharlal Nehru, 15 June 1924, *A Bunch of Old Letters*, p. 37.

led by Gandhi, was reluctant to resolve the communal impasse and allowed the 'Lala-Malaviya gang' to pursue their communal ends. 'We who worked for ten years through thick and thin with Gandhiji pressed action upon him, but the desire of retaining Hindu popularity for himself and for Pandit Motilal Nehru prevented a settlement', complained Mohamed Ali.[46] He was also distressed by the growing fissures in the Hindu-Muslim alliance cemented by the ingenious C.R. Das, the strains in the Punjab Unionist Party caused by the overtly anti-Muslim Arya Samajists and Hindu Mahasabhites, the revival and intensification of the *shuddhi* and *sangathan* movements, and the role of some leading Congressmen in perpetuating communal discord. Commenting on the Delhi riot of July 1924 specifically, but on the deteriorating communal situation generally, Mohamed Ali wrote: 'And pray Mahatmaji forgive a pang of sorrow, the cry of a well-nigh broken heart, the credit of it all goes, in the first instance, to the misguided spirit of the *sangathan* movement, and the superfluous boastings of the *shuddhi* leaders . . . . .I feel sick, positively sick of it all'.[47] But Gandhi and his comrades paid no heed to Mohamed Ali's repeated protestations for immediate remedial measures in the wake of widespread communal violence. It is doubtful if the Gandhian initiatives would have yielded results, but it may have revitalised the dampen spirits of his Muslim followers and encouraged them to pursue their campaign against the communal forces. Instead, Gandhi chose to give precedence to untouchability and the spinning wheel over the Hindu-Muslim problem, admitted his own imperfection as an instrument for bringing about communal peace, conveniently maintained in his characteristically saintly fashion that the 'Hindu-Muslim problem had passed out of human hands into God's, hand's [8] and rationalised his inactivity by writing in May 1927:

> I wish I could do something but I am utterly helpless. My faith in unity is as bright as ever; only I see no daylight out of the impenetrable darkness. I cry out to God for light.[49]

46 Quoted in Qureshi, *Ulema in Politics*, p. 298.
47 Mohamed Ali to Gandhi, 21 July 1924, MAP.
48 Quoted in B.R. Nanda, *Mahatma Gandhi* (London, 1959), p. 259.
49 Cited in S.K. Majumdar, *Jinnah and Gandhi* (Calcutta, 1966), p. 139. Later, in response to Jinnah's 'Fourteen Points', he wrote in a similar strain.

Such an expression, which appears pathetic in retrospect, dampened the cause of Hindu-Muslim amity and tended to eventuate into communal attitudes. They also weakened the faith which some influential Muslims reposed in Gandhi's leadership and in the efficacy of his methods, and shattered their confidence in the Congress as the champion of communal harmony. Evidence of growing disillusionment is to be found in the correspondence of Mohamed Ali, Abdul Bari, Ansari, Khaliquzzaman, T.A.K. Sherwani, and Syed Mahmud. In February 1930, Ansari pleaded with Gandhi not to launch civil disobedience which, in the circumstances then prevailing, was bound to unleash forces destructive of Hindu-Muslim unity. In his view the country was not ready for civil disobedience because Hindu-Muslim unity had reached its 'lowest water-mark' by contrast with the communal fraternization of 1920, and Sikhs were almost entirely against Congress whereas then they had been firm supporters. Moreover, the Congress was a divided organization and there were clear signs of overt revolt, 'diversity of purpose, complete lack of enthusiasm among the workers', and the virtual certainty of violent outbreaks'. To embark on civil disobedience in such a situation would 'do an incalculable damage'.[50] Expressing his disagreement with Ansari and stating the prudence of his programme, Gandhi wrote on 16 February that he could not turn back now. He agreed that the Hindu-Muslim problem was fundamental, but felt that it had to be approached differently—'not at present by adjustment of the political power but by one or the other acting on the square under all circumstances'. Political adjustment was only possible if there was some trust between the two communities and Congress could only command such trust

> by becoming fearless and strictly just. But meanwhile the third party—the evil British power—has got to be sterilized. There will be no charter of independence before the Hindus

'My mind is in a whirl in this matter. The atmosphere is too foggy for me to see clearly'. Gandhi to Motilal Nehru, 12 August 1929, Motilal Nehru Papers (G-1), NML.

50 Ansari to Gandhi, 13 February 1930, in Hasan (ed.), *Muslims and the Congress*, pp. 99-100.

> and the Muslims have met but there can be virtual independence before the charter is received.[51]

Ansari was perturbed by Gandhi's reply. So were his nationalist Muslim colleagues. Khaliquzzaman, for instance, regretted that Gandhi did not consider Hindu-Muslim unity as an essential preliminary for a fight for independence. 'If we accept the formula, laid down therein', he wrote, 'we indirectly proclaim to the Muslim community to find its champions in people who believe that communalism in India is a fact'.[52] Syed Mahmud also wrote of the danger of civil disobedience erupting into communal riots. He, too, asked for advice, torn between loyalty to Jawaharlal Nehru and dislike of the policy, reinforced by his need to earn a living at the Bar.[53] Ansari could do nothing except to advice his colleagues to remain in the Congress because there was no other political option. 'We must not leave the Congress', he pleaded with T.A.K. Sherwani, 'nor must we do anything to weaken the Congress. . .To leave the Congress would be to commit suicide, to oppose the Congress would be a crime'.[5]

Such pious sentiments could hardly allay widespread Muslim fear that Swaraj in Congress terms meant Hindu domination. In fact, it is hardly surprising that several Muslim groups, including the Nationalist Muslims, began to question the assumption that Congress was friendly towards them and that the best way to protect their interests was to join the civil disobedience movement. This was best articulated by Haji Hidayet Hosain, one of the founders of the Muslim League and a leading figure in UP politics. The Haji expressed his misgivings, shared by many of his contemporaries, in response to Ansari's circular to attend the Madras session of the Congress in December 1927. The Haji wrote:

> It is admitted on all hands that no political advancement is possible till the Hindus and the Muslims unite; what have even the Congressmen done to secure this unity. Indeed some of the Congress workers have been the worst offenders in this

51 Gandhi to Ansari, 16 February 1930, *ibid.*, p. 101.
52 Khaliquzzaman to Ansari, 1 March 1930, *ibid.*, p. 110.
53 Syed Mahmud to Ansari, n.d., *ibid.*, p. 106.
54 Ansari to T.A.K. Sherwani, 6 January 1930, *ibid.*, p. 90.

respect. Has the Congress even as a body attempted to go to the root cause of the Hindu-Muslim riots ? Have you realised that it is only since 1923, when the *shuddhi* and *sangathan* were started, that these riots began to repeat themselves with such frequent obstinacy ? Nobody has got a right to take exception to these movements but if the object of the *shuddhi* were merely political and pursued by physical force, threat, violence and fraud in order to reduce the numerical strength of the Muslims, then I think these movements can secure no other purpose except the creation of an unbridgeable gulf between the two communities. . . .

Mere honeyed phrases and appeals couched in eloquent and winsome phraseology to the communities to live in amity and grace has never proved to be of any avail. You cry in the wilderness every year and this year you repeat the same process over again. It may do your soul some good, but it does nothing to us. The Congress does not represent the Hindus now, it has never represented the Muslims. You are then a group of men, well meaning, well intentioned, honest and sincere, but all the same afraid to look at things at their face, incapable of tapping the root cause of differences and therefore impotent to devise effective means of cure.[55]

This was strong language. The Haji knew this. He confessed that he was being impertinent. But he was stating, as well as it was possible for a contemporary, unendowed with the advantage of hindsight, the tangled state of communal prejudices that seemed to inspire people either with cynicism or with wooly idealism.[56]

55 Hidayet Hosain to Ansari, 12 December 1927, *ibid.*, pp. 41-42.

56 These lines are borrowed from the review of *Muslims and the Congress* by Sudhir Chandra. See *Indian Archives*, May-June 1980, p. 74.

5

THE NEHRU REPORT: DEBATE AND CRUSADE

The publication of the Nehru Committee Report set in motion the avalanche of Mohamed Ali's eloquence against Gandhi and the Congress. In view of the significance of his criticism and its impact on the Muslims, the recommendations of the Nehru Report merit consideration.[1]

The Nehru Committee Report was published on 15 August 1928. It was an impressive document which covered a wide range of constitutional issues. An introductory chapter made out a case for full Dominion Status while three chapters dealt with the communal problem. The final recommendations, which bore the impression of a considerable amount of labour and thought, were given in chapter seven. These included proposals relating to reservation of seats, the form of electorate, and the future status of Sind and the North-West Frontier Province. In addition to this, there was a Declaration of Rights which guaranteed religious liberty and cultural autonomy to each individual and group. It aimed at allaying Muslim fears of Hindu domination. 'We cannot have one community domineering over another', declared the report.

The Nehru Report conceded some of the Muslim demands embodied in the Delhi Proposals, formulated by some Muslim leaders in March 1927. Motilal Nehru, Chairman of the Committee which drafted the report, persuaded M.S. Aney and Mangal Singh, who represented the Hindu Mahasabha and the Sikh League

1 This section is based on my study of the Nehru Report in *Nationalism and Communal Politics in India*, pp. 275-280.

respectively, to agree to the separation of Sind from Bombay and its elevation, in company with the North-West Frontier Province, to the status of full province. The report, however, rejected the Muslim demand for reservation of seats in Bengal and the Punjab. Its verdict was that reservation of seats for majorities was 'incompatible with real representative and responsible government'. However, on the basis of statistics provided by Jawaharlal Nehru and Subhas Chandra Bose, the report concluded that the Bengali and Punjabi Muslims did not require any 'adventitious aid' to secure the full benefit of their natural majority. Their population was so distributed that in whatever way the electorates were formed, they were sure of capturing a majority of seats in the legislative councils and local bodies. And finally, the argument that the Hindus who were a minority in population in the Punjab and Bengal but were a majority in voting registers ceased to have any validity under a system of adult franchise recommended by the Nehru Report.

In the Hindu-majority provinces, however, the authors of the Nehru Report were compelled by 'force of circumstances to introduce a temporary element of communalism' in the form of reservation of seats for Muslim minorities in proportion to their population both in the central and the provincial legislatures. This meant that the weightage fixed for Muslims under the Lucknow Pact and the Montagu-Chelmsford Reforms was done away with. Separate electorates were also abolished. According to the report, the principle of weightage had no place in joint or mixed electorates:

> It is of course not physically impossible to reserve a large proportion of seats for Muslim minorities than their population would justify but, apart from the obvious injustice of such a course not only to majorities but to the minorities as well, it will in our opinion be harmful to the development of Muslims themselves on national lines. We have allowed them their full share on the population basis by reservation and over and above that share they must win by their own effort. We do not propose to impose any restrictions on their right to contest a large number of seats than those reserved for them.

And finally, there was the thorny question of Muslim representation in the central legislature. Muslims claimed that their population-one-third of the total-entitled them to a similar proportion of seats in the central legislature. Their population, however, was so unevenly distributed that they could not be certain of securing one-third of the members by election. They, therefore, demanded that one-third of the seats be reserved for their community. This argument was pursued by Shuaib Qureshi at the All-Parties Conference and unanimously adopted by the All-India Muslim League and its povincial branches. But, with the exception of Tej Bahadur Sapru, no member of the Nehru Committee accepted this demand. In fact, it was maintained that Muslims formed less than one-fourth of the total population of British India and were not entitled to reservation over and above that proportion in the central legislature.

In sum, then, the Nehru Report recommended reservation of seats for Muslims only in provinces where they were in a minority. By a stroke of pen its authors abolished separate electorates, discarded reservation of seats for Muslim majorities in the Punjab and Bengal, and rejected the principle of weightage for Muslim minorities. This was an extraordinary decision in the light of the Lucknow Pact and the subsequent Congress-League negotiations. In May 1927, Motilal Nehru and Srinivasa Iyengar had taken the lead in persuading Congress to accept the Delhi Proposals which contained the provision for one-third representation in the central legislature as well as reservation of seats for the Muslim majority in Bengal and the Punjab. So, why did Motilal and his Congress colleagues perform a *volte face*? Was it intended to undo the 'wrongs' done to Hindus in UP and the Punjab by the Lucknow Pact? Or, did Motilal and other Hindu Congressmen succumb to the Hindu Mahasabha pressures, as alleged by some Muslims? To answer these questions, we must examine the reactions of leading Hindu politicians to the Nehru Report.

To many Hindus, the report was 'the most authoritative statement and exposition of national demands', and the recommendations relating to the communal problem were 'bold, outspoken and fearless'. The great merit of the report, was that, unlike the Lucknow Pact, it did not propose any abrupt changes in the relative position of the various communities in the legislatures. In the Hindu-majority provinces, in particular, there was relief at the abolition of separate electorates and weightage for Muslims. The same was true of the Punjabi and Bengali Hindus who had consistently campaigned against the reservation of seats accorded to the Muslim majorities by the Lucknow Pact. Thus Lala Lajpat Rai, who was one of the important leaders in the campaign, urged his followers to accept the Nehru Report. So did the leaders of the Arya Samaj Sabha like Raja Narendranath and Gulshan Rai.

While preparing the report, Motilal and his other colleagues could not have ignored the strength of Hindu opposition to the Lucknow Pact. They must have realized that an attempt to prepare an agreement on similar lines would alienate Hindus from the Congress and drive them into the Hindu Mahasabha camp. So, the only way of taking the steam out of the Hindu Sabha campaign and of gaining widespread Hindu support for the Nehru Report was to reject those terms of the Lucknow Pact which were unpopular amongst Hindus in Punjab and UP.

As regards Muslims, Motilal assumed that the introduction of adult suffrage would satisfy them in Bengal and the Punjab, and the detailed statistics on their performance in the district board elections would allay their fears of Hindu domination. This assumption was not without a basis. Motilal's hopes that the Nehru Report would be welcomed by Muslims in the Punjab and Bengal came true. The UP Muslims, on the other hand, did not figure prominently in his calculations. He was confident of gaining the support of the Nationalist Muslims, but for the rest he showed no concern. He was convinced that if the Punjabi and Bengali Muslims were won over, Muslims elsewhere 'would be settled by throwing a few crumbs here and there'. In this case, Motilal's expectations were not fulfilled. The UP Muslims, who men he expected would settle for a few crumbs, eventually led a massive agitation against the Nehru Report and even succeeded in enticing away its Muslim supporters in other provinces. Over the years, they remained in the forefront of the Muslim separatist movement and were, indeed, the architects of Pakistan. The controversy over the Nehru Report initiated a debate which was resolved only in 1947 with tragic consequences.

II

Mohamed Ali objected to the Nehru Report for several reasons. In the first place, he assailed its authors for discarding the demand for complete independence, though a year later he was purposefully vague in stating that, 'while I am *not* committed to a refusal of *Dominion Status* at once, I cannot commit myself to an abhorrence of *Independence* either. . . .For my part I am prepared to accept Dominion Status'.[2] In response to the Nehru Report, however, he categorically rejected Dominion Status which was 'inconsistent with the independent spirit of Islam'.[3] At the All-India Khilafat Conference, held in Calcutta on 25 December 1928, Mohamed Ali said: 'Today Mahatma Gandhi and Sir Ali Imam would be sitting under our flag and over them would fly the flag of the Union Jack. The Nehru Report in its preamble has admitted the bondage of servitude'.[4] In the days of the East India Company, the beat of drum was accompanied by the cry "Creation is God's, the country is the King's, and the rule is that of John Company Bahadur". The Nehru Report, according to Mohamed Ali, meant that the creation was God's, the country was the Viceroy's or of the Parliament's and the rule was Hindu Mahasabha's.[5]

Another criticism was that the Nehru Report discarded federalism and recommended a unitary central government. This was inconsistent with the Muslim League demand for a decentralised federal government with residuary powers being vested in the component provinces, a demand which aimed to ensure that a 'Hindu-dominated central legislature' would not legislate against 'Muslim interests'. At the same time, the Nehru Report proposed Muslim representation in the central legislature at 25 per cent and not 33 per cent as claimed by the Muslim League and the All-India Muslim Conference, held in March 1927. This was outrageous. Mohamed spoke indignantly: You make compromises

2 Mohamed Ali to Jinnah, 16 January 1930, MAP.

3 At a public meeting in Bombay on 11 August 1929, he said:

> We are depicted in the Hindu and the so-called Nationalist Press as shirkers of our duty and responsibility even by men who had never made any sacrifice. The records of 1919 and 1921 bear witness to the courage and sacrifice of Muslims and yet today, when we demand our rights, the monopolists turn round, abuse and misrepresent us. We had accepted the Madras resolution on independence as our goal. Compare this with what the Nehru Report offers us. It is only meant to perpetuate slavery and Hindu domination. *India Quarterly Register*, July-December 1929, vol. 2, pp. 352-353.

4 *Ibid*., July-December 1928, vol. 2, p. 402.

5 Speech at the Bihar and Orissa All-Parties Conference, 9 December 1928, *ibid*., p. 426.

in your constitution every day with false doctrines, immoral conception and wrong ideas, 'but you make no compromise with our communalists—with separate electorates and reserve seats. Twenty-five per cent is our proportion of the population and yet you will not give us 33 per cent in the Assembly. You are a Jew, a bania'.[6]

Separate electorates and weightages were two other crucial issues which figured in Mohamed Ali's outburst against the Nehru Report. He had consistently regarded separate electorates as a cornerstone of Muslim political demands because 'it prevented a small minority from being swamped by an overwhelming majority'.[7] 'The principle of communal electorates', he observed in the *Comrade* of 22 January 1926:

> is a confession of our failure in winning the confidence of minorities, and it would cease only when the majority proves not by its words, with which it is ever free but by its acts, that it is not only Hindu, but Indian also.[8]

As regards weightage in any future representative system, UP Muslims justified their claim in terms of their past historical and political importance rather than in terms of their numbers. The Lucknow Pact recognised this in December 1916; the Nehru Report rejected it. Mohamed Ali was indignat. Without weightage, he said, 'Muslims would be subservient everywhere and Hindus would be able to establish a 'a legalised tyranny of numbers'.[9] This was an exaggerated fear, at least in the context of the UP where Muslims occupied an important position in public service and the professions.[10] Yet, the dichotomy between the objective reality and the subjective perception of various groups gave

6 *Indian Quarterly Register*, *op. cit.*, p, 403.

7 In the first issue of the *Comrade*, he declared that 'separate electorates have been found to be necessary at this state exactly because there exist at present distinct and well-defined Hindu and Muslim standpoints in regard to the common, immediate and everyday affairs of Indian life'. *Comrade*, 11 January 1911. Also, 28 January 1911, 29 March 1913, 19 January and 6 February 1925; Iqbal (ed.), *Writings and Speeches*, pp. 362-361.

8 *Ibid.*, 22 January 1926,

9 Jafri (ed.), *Nigarishat-i-Mohamed Ali*, vol. 2, p. 23.

10 Paul Brass, *Language, Religion and Politics in North India* (Cambridge, 1974); Robinson, *Separatism among Indian Muslims*.

credence to the apprehensions voiced by Mohamed Ali. This was particularly so in the case of government servants and landowners who, having gained positions of power and influence through separate electorates and government nomination, now faced the cheerless prospect of losing their seats in legislative bodies. There was another danger. The proposal of adult suffrage, if accepted by government, meant the further enfranchisement of over fifteen million voters, mainly tenants: so the landlords faced the possibility of being ousted from the general constituencies as well. Malcolm Hailey informed the Chairman of the Statutory Commission that:

> Curiously enough, the Nehru Committee's Report is likely to work in our favour, for the landowners are not unnaturally perturbed at the prospect of adult suffrage and the abolition of the reserved seats which they now hold.[11]

In consequence, men like Nawab Jamshed Ali Khan, president of the Muzaffarnagar Zamindar Association, the Raja of Jahangirabad, an affluent taluqdar from Barabanki district, Shafa'at Ahmad Khan and Shaikh Abdullah, identified as 'independent conservatives', submitted a memorandum to the Statutory Commission on behalf of the 'Muslims of the United Provinces'. Consistent with their earlier stance, they opposed all forms of provincial advance if their position was not safeguarded, and criticised the abolition of the nominated element and special constituencies. Their demands included separate electorates with weightages at every level of government, and effective Muslim representation on all autonomous institutions created by the legislatures.[12]

Mohamed Ali joined this well-orchestrated campaign against the Nehru Report, combining with Khilafat leaders like Haji Abdullah Haroon of Sind and Shafi Daudi of Bihar, to wean away its Muslim supporters. But their efforts were successful only in Bombay where the Muslim League, consisting of seventy-one members,[13] rejected the report on account of the inadequate

11 Hailey to Simon, 28 August 1928, Hailey Papers (13-B).

12 See Hasan, *Nationalism and Communal Politics*, pp. 291-92.

13 'List of the members of the Bombay Presidency Muslim League,' M.C. Chagla Papers, NML.

provisions for the 'proper and efficient protection and safeguards' of Muslim interests.[14] In Bihar, Bengal and the Punjab, on the other hand, they met with stiff resistance from the Muslim supporters of the Nehru Report.[15] In UP Mohamed Ali's crusade suffered a setback when he failed to get elected as president of the Muslim League. The victory of his arch rival, the Raja of Mahmudabad, signalled the triumph of the pro-Report lobby.[16]

Towards the end of December 1928, Mohamed Ali and his cohorts made yet another attempt to turn the tables against their opponents. The first opportunity arose at the Khilafat Committee meeting on 21 December, which met to elect delegates for the All-India Khilafat Conference. The Ali Brothers, in league with Shafi Daudi, disrupted the meeting which was overwhelmingly in favour of the Nehru Report and had their own list of delegates adopted. They employed similar 'methods of obstruction and procrastination' at the Central Khilafat Committee meeting, which led to the resignation of many delegates and their subsequent boycott of the All-India Khilafat Conference, presided over by Mohamed Ali. A few days later, Mohamed Ali attended the All-Parties Muslim Conference at Delhi, convened by the pro-government lobby and their allies in the Assembly and the legislative councils.

At the Conference, controversies over Dominion Status or Independence, cow-slaughter, music before mosque, and about the boycott of the Statutory Commission were thrust aside because they were regarded as subsidiary to the fundamental question of Muslim safeguards in any future devolution of power. The main resolution passed at the conference called for a federation with complete autonomy and residuary powers being vested in the constituent states. It also detailed the demands for separate electorates, for weightages in legislatures and local bodies, for a due share in public services, for the separation of Sind from Bombay Presidency, and for the establishment of provincial governments

14 Irwin to Peel, 12 December 1928, Irwin Papers (152-4).

15 *Bombay Chronicle*, 6, 17 November 1928.

16 The Raja of Mahmudabad was a keen supporter of the Nehru Report. He was a signatory to a manifesto issued in its favour by the Nationalist Muslims—M.A. Ansari, Saifuddin Kitchlew, Zafar Ali Khan, Syed Mahmud, Khaliquzzaman, M.C. Chagla, and Yaqub Hasan of Madras. *Ibid.*, 26 October 1928.

in Sind, the North-West Frontier Province, and Baluchistan. The Conference emphatically declared that 'no constitution, by whomsoever proposed or devised', was acceptable to Indian Muslims unless it conformed with the principles embodied in its resolution.[17] 'It is a tragedy of Indian public life', lamented the *Servants of India*, 'that Mohamed Ali . . . seconded these demands and made an exceedingly truculent speech in [their] support. One's heart sinks at the thought that the Ali Brothers should have been among the staunchest supporters of the Conference.'[18] Ansari was particularly disappointed because his ceaseless efforts to come to an understanding with Mohamed Ali and his friends came to nothing. Expressing his anguish and surprise at their parleys with the 'Aga Khan and Co', Ansari wrote:

> Ever since the Lucknow Convention many of us have been making ceaseless efforts to come to an understanding with the Ali Brothers and their friends. We tried at Lucknow, then at Patna and then finally at Calcutta, but we failed. Not only that. They gradually but surely went on receding from us until at last they found themselves in the company of the Aga Khan and Sir Mohammad Shafi in January last. The willingness with which they associated themselves with people whose only distinction is that they have always been reactionary in regard both to Indian and Muslim affairs was surprising. Mohamed Ali actually seconded the resolution proposed by Sir Mohammad Shafi at the All-Parties Muslim Conference in Delhi. The Ali Brothers still stand by that resolution which no sensible Indian can entertain seriously but which they regard as the minimum of Muslim demands. . .
>
> Indeed the differences that in their origin concerned a few provisions of the Nehru Report have now grown into a conflict of the very outlook. This to my mind explained why the Ali Brothers are adopting an irreconcilable attitude although they know very well that they are thereby strengthening the government as well as the communalists, both Hindu and Muslim. . .[19]

17 *Times of India*, 3 January 1929.

18 *Servants of India*, 10 January 1929.

19 Ansari to Mazharul Haq, 7 September 1929, Hasan (ed.), *Muslims and the Congress*, pp. 86-87.

A striking feature of the Conference was the spirit of unanimity which prevailed amongst the participants. Mohamed Ali sat beside Mohammad Shafi whom he had so often derided as a government stooge, and the Aga Khan was cheered by Azad Sobhani whose vitriolic speeches at Kanpur in 1913 had forced him to resign from the Muslim League. The combination of these individuals and their followers reflected the changing course in the stream of Muslim separatist politics.

The Delhi Conference was followed by a series of meetings and informal discussions which sought to restore unity among the self-styled leaders of the Muslim community, and to replace rival Leagues and Associations by a central organisation which would 'try and faithfully reflect Muslim desires and aspirations'.[20] The efforts bore fruit, and, on 24 March 1929, the 'Delhi Manifesto' was issued by 20 Muslim leaders, including Jinnah, Mohammad Shafi, and the Ali Brothers. The signatories urged Muslims not to take part in meetings and processions organised by the Congress because its leaders were bent on bolstering up the Nehru Report which the Muslims repudiated in no uncertain fashion.[21]

Jawaharlal Nehru reacted angrily to Mohamed Ali's signing the 'Delhi Manifesto'. He declared it as a 'treason' against Congress by one who had served as its president. But Mohamed Ali was equally vehement in his denunciation of leading Congressmen and their policies. In a sharp rebuttal to Jawaharlal, he condemned Congress leaders like Malaviya for defying the party's decisions in respect of non-cooperation, non-violence, Hindu-Muslim unity and the removal of untouchability. As a price of his cooperation, Malaviya 'wanted to place a revolver in the hands of every Hindu lady, no doubt as a token of non-violence, and of course all the Hindu-Muslim riots in which he has never said a word against Hindus are in full conformity with the Congress precepts of Hindu-Muslim unity'. Likewise, he chided Motilal Nehru for defying the Congress resolutions against council entry and for 'killing non-cooperation just as he is killing the Congress today and merging it into the Hindu Mahasabha in spite of his well known lack of Hindu orthodoxy'.[22]

20 *Times of India*, 5 March 1929.
21 *Ibid.*, 8 March 1929.
22 *Ibid.*, 19 March 1929.

III

The publication of the Nehru Report, quite evidently, deepened Mohamed Ali's hostility towards Congress and turned him into its most uncompromising critic. The Congress, he came to believe, was no longer a national organization but a Hindu one. unprepared to condemn those Hindu fanatics who were perpetuating communal discord, and unprepared to work towards the creation of an India in which all communities could live in harmony.[23] His participation in the All-Parties Muslim Conference, organised by overtly communal Muslims, signalled his complete alienation from the Congress. His relationship with Gandhi, forged largely on the principle of expediency, also suffered severe strains. Differences arose over a large number of issues, particularly those relating to the causes of Hindu-Muslim discord, leading to mutual acrimination.[24] Mohamed Ali deplored Gandhi's fervent campaigning for the Nehru Report and quoted from his writings of 1924 and 1925 to show that the Mahatma was now converted to a different creed and was striving for different goals. He wrote to this effect:

> Gandhi has defeated all Muslim attempts for a compromise. He is giving free reins to the communalism of the majority. The Nehru constitution is the legalised tyranny of numbers and is the way to rift and not peace. It recognises the rank communalism of the majority as nationalism. The safeguards proposed to limit the high-handedness of the majority are branded as communal.[25]

The gulf that separated Gandhi and Mohamed Ali seemed unbridgeable; by 1928, their relationship reached a breaking point. Gandhi conceded that the Ali Brothers 'had a fairly heavy list of complaints', against him and that he could not make an 'impression on

23 Mohamed Ali, 'Hindu-Muslim Ta'aluqat awr Maslak-i-Khilafat', in Jafri (ed.), *Maqalat*, vol. 2, pp. 137-146.

24 A most useful account of these differences is provided by Mohibbul Hasan, 'Mahatma Gandhi and the Indian Muslims', S.C. Biswas (ed.), *Gandhi Theory and Practice: Social Impact and Contemporary Relevance* (Simla, 1969).

25 *Nigarishat-i-Mohamed Ali*, quoted in Abdul Hamid, *Muslim Separatism in India, 1858-1947* (Karachi, 1971 edn.), p. 201.

them as they distrust the role of my associates'.[26] This was confirmed by Mohamed Ali's outburst in April 1930 at the communally-oriented Muslim Conference, organised by one of the chief architects of Muslim separatist politics—the redoubtable Aga Khan. 'We refuse to join Mr. Gandhi', stated Gandhi's lieutenant during the Khilafat and non-cooperation days, 'because his movement [civil disobedience] is not a movement for complete independence of India but for making the seventy millions of Indian Muslims dependent on the Hindu Mahasabha'.[27] The country, he argued, was not prepared to undertake civil disobedience: it lacked unity, discipline and self-control. He also expressed doubt as to whether Gandhi would stick to his own programme:

> Doubtless man who could suddenly call off the Non-cooperation campaign at Bardoli in 1922, with the same astonishing about-face can inaugurate a civil disobedience movement in 1930. But what surety is there that he would not again order suspension, just as he did eight years ago, only a few days after serving an ultimatum to the Viceroy.[28]

Symbolic of the collapse of the old alliance on which Gandhi had built non-cooperation was Mohamed Ali's appeal to Muslims not to join civil disobedience because its goal was Hindu raj. He also advised them to send delegations to London to put forward their demands, and expressed his own willingness to cooperate. To the Viceroy, he wrote:

> While I deny the right of any but Indians themselves to shape their destinies, I am not only willing but anxious to proceed to England, along with other representatives of Indian communities, parties and interests, to confer with the representatives of Great Britain and persuade them to recognise India's natural demand for self-determination.[29]

26 Gandhi to Motilal Nehru, 12 August 1229, Motilal Nehru Papers (G-1), NML.

27 Quoted in Reginald Coupland, *The Constitutional Problem in India* (Oxford, 1944), Pt. 3, p. 111.

28 Jafri (ed.), *Nigarishat-i-Mohamed Ali*, pp. 237-72, quoted in Watson, *op.cit.*, p. 92.

29 Mohamed Ali to Irwin, 11 September 1930, MAP.

Furthermore, the Ali Brothers tried to exert pressure on the *Jamiyat-i-ulama*, a pro-Congress organization from the non-cooperation days, to reverse its decision, taken at the Amroha Conference in May 1930, to support civil disobedience.[30] The Nawab of Bhopal, aghast at the Amroha resolution, reported the following developments to the Viceroy:

> In my letter to Your Excellency I had forecasted a split in the Jamiat and it did take place. The Ali Brothers with a strong and influential body of ulemas [sic] have definitely started a new Jamiat-ul-Ulema . . They have advised the Muslims to keep aloof from the present struggle and to dissociate themselves from the Congress . . .The new Jamiat is also in favour of participation in the Round Table Conference.[31]

Reporting on the 'remnants of the old Jamiat who have been bought over by the Congress', the Nawab wrote that they

> are divided amongst themselves and disruptive forces are already at work. But even the rump dropped the question of *Fatwa* altogether and the resolution they finally adopted is too confused, halting and hesitating to do very much harm. In the struggle that is bound to follow between the two Jamiat—the old and the new—I see possibilities of doing something to mend the situation. It is not yet possible to foretell with any degree of precision the course of development of a rather complex situation. But I am sending a competent and trusted person to study the question further and to exercise a sobering influence on the unbalanced minds of the old Jamiat . . . .[32]

So the Mahatma's hope that, 'if truth is in me, the Brothers must capitulate' remained unfulfilled.[33] At a public meeting in Bombay on 11 August 1929, Mohamed Ali accused Gandhi of 'working under the influence of the communalist Hindu Mahasabha',

30 Maulana Al-Hafiz and A.H. Siddiqi, *Jamiyat-i-ulama ke chand eham Khidmat-i-milli* (Delhi, 1940), p. 9.

31 The Nawab of Bhopal to Irwin, 10 May 1930, Irwin Papers (152/24).

32 *Ibid.*

33 *Young India*, 3 April 1930, *CWG*, vol. 43, p. 126.

and 'fighting for the supremacy of Hinduism and submergence of Muslims'.[34] This was strong language used by the fiery and impetuous Mohamed Ali; it reflected his complete estrangement from Gandhi and from the Congress. But he had clearly gone too far in his denunciation of Gandhi and in his repudiation of Congress policies. The vehemence of his attack, while certain to alienate many of his political friends like M.A. Ansari, was not certain to attract new support; in fact its immediate effect seems to have been even to increase his unpopularity. His moving speech at the Round Table Conference in November 1930 appeared to be the raving of a man isolated, inconsolably bereaved, dying, yet rejoicing in his incomparable power to express his fury in words whose sheer exuberance is still astounding. 'I want to go back to my country', Mohamed Ali declared, 'with the substance of freedom in my hand. Otherwise I will not go back to a slave country. I would even prefer to die in a foreign country so long as it is a free country, and if you do not give me freedom in India you will have to give me a grave here'. Somewhat inconsistently, he added that if the delegates returned to India without freedom, they would return to an America, to a lost dominion, where they would build not a United States, but a 'United Faiths' of India.[35]

IV

It is evident that the fears generated by Mohamed Ali's virulent campaign against the Nehru Report provided material for Muslim

34 Jafri (ed.), *Selections from Mohamed Ali's Comrade*, p. 202. In an obvious reference to Gandhi and his other critics he said:

> People who run down the Ali Brothers and the Khilafat Committee as communalists and pride themselves on their nationalism—let them know what we communalists think and how low we think of their nationalism . . . . Islam means peace and nationalism means war. God made Islam to link all mankind in one family and one community. This is my communalism. All mankind is divided into nations each being the enemy of others. That is your nationalism, which leads to war . . . You have the Union Jack over in one link of servitude and bondage with England and yet your ideal of nationalism is to divide mankind into enemies, but my ideal is to unite man with man without sword or force. My communalism is to bring all into the fold of Islam by love, persuasion and service.

India Quarterly Register, July-December, 1928, vol. 2, p, 403.

35 Watson, *op. cit.*, p. 93.

politicians in search of potent rallying cries. Also, his analysis of the Congress movement became the central plank of a propaganda battle which raged throughout the course of civil disobedience. In the new situation, the potential of his name was recognised by the government; so the Viceroy, at the suggestion of the Governor of Bombay, nominated him as a delegate to the Round Table Conference. 'He is one of the ablest Mohammadan I have met', wrote Frederick Sykes, 'and still has great influence with his community. I feel that it would be much easier to deal with him in the Conference than outside it'.[36] The organisers of the All-Parties Muslim Conference, indirectly encouraged by the government, also pinned their hopes in Mohamed Ali, egging him to press the 'Fourteen Points' of M.A. Jinnah and insisting that he attend the Round Table Conference in order to articulate the political aspirations of his community. 'The basis of these [fourteen points] is separate electorates', wrote Ameer Ali. He added:

> If any form of joint electorate is introduced, whatever the safeguards may be, you will never get an independent Muslim elected again to the Legislature. . .*Be true to your constituents in India. You are not taking part in a bargain but in moulding the future for yourselves and your children* (emphasis added).[37]

Mohamed Ali concurred. He joined the Muslim delegation to London, led by the Aga Khan, with the firm conviction that critical collaboration with the government in the Round Table Conference would bring more political benefits than sedition in Congress company. But his departure from India was marked by gloom, for he knew that his mission was condemned as traitorous by those people with whom he had worked in the past.[38]

To counteract Mohamed Ali's opposition to civil disobedience and to integrate Muslims into the movement, the Congress made special appeals to Muslims to cooperate. The working committee passed a resolution in June 1930 reiterating its Lahore pledge (December 1929) that it would accept no solution to the communal

36 Sykes to Irwin, 16 May 1930, Sykes Papers MSS. EUR. F. 150(2-A), IOL.
37 Ameer Ali to Mohamed Ali, 9 December 1930, MAP.
38 Watson, *op. cit.*, p. 93.

problem which was unacceptable to Muslims.[39] At the same time, members of the Ahrar and Khaksar movements, the *Jamiyat-i-ulama*, the Nationalist Muslim Party, and the *Khudai Khidmatgars*, led by Khan Abdul Ghaffar Khan, were pressed into service in order to enlist Muslim support and to rebut accusations of Muslim apathy. Appeals were also made in the name of religion,[40] with Congress workers often trying to exploit Muslim sympathy for their brethren in Palestine, Turkey and Egypt. 'Can Muslim hearts ring true and yet allow this Government to make cowards and weaklings of us all ? Can the hand that ravages Palestine, tyrannises Egypt, harassed Turkey, be the protecting one for, the Indian Muslims ? Will our Muslim comrades be taken in by the Simon bluff ?'[41]

Such appeals had no impact on the Muslims who, in marked contrast to the non-cooperation days, showed no inclination to join civil disobedience. This was noticeable in Bengal,[42] and in the Punjab where, according to the All India Congress Committee (AICC) Report, 'communal tension and preoccupation with communal affairs and controversies raised serious impediments in the path of the Congress'.[43] Bombay was no different.[44] A Congress

39 J.M. Brown, *Gandhi and Civil Disobedience: The Mahatma in Indian Politics 1928-1934* (Cambridge, 1977), p. 149.

40 For example, the controversy over the Sarda Act figured prominently in attempts to enlist Muslim support. The Congress workers sought to capitalise on Muslim resentment towards the Sarda Act. Viceroy to Secretary of State, 11 May 1930, Home Poll. 1930, 483, NAI.

41 Bulletin of the Bombay Satyagraha Committee, 11 June 1930, R.E. Hawkins Papers, Centre for South Asian Studies, Cambridge.

42 In Jessore, for instance, a meeting under the presidency of Mujibur Rahman, editor of *Mussalman*, in support of civil disobedience was broken up by a group of Muslims FR (Bengal) Home poll. 1900, 248 and K.W., NAI. For further evidence of Muslim opposition to civil disobedience, see Tanika Sarkar, 'The First Phase of Civil Disobedience in Bengal, 1930-1,' *Indian Historical Review*, July 1977; Kenneth Mcpherson, *The Muslim Microcosm: Calcutta, 1918 to 1935* (Wiesbaden, 1974), pp. 113-116.

43 AICC Papers (G/3), 1932.

44 The *Anjuman-i-Islam*, a leading Muslim organization in Bombay, declared its opposition to civil disobedience. In August 1930, the Governor of Bombay was satisfied that 'the Muhammadans are giving no trouble and show no inclination to join the Congress. Their leaders appear to be hoping to achieve a considerable proportion of their aims at the Round

meeting on 11 June 1930 ended in a complete fiasco, with the Muslim audience refusing to listen to a Muslim speaker who sought to convince them of the virtues of civil disobedience. Not very long afterwards, the Muslims of Bombay accorded a very different reception to Shaukat Ali, when he told them to completely dissociate themselves from civil disobedience[45] and warned Congress leaders that if picketting and boycott against Muslim merchants continued, 'peace would become impossible and this woud be the beginning of much greater strife than we have witnessed'.[46] The Muslims of Bombay, responding in no uncertain terms, asserted themselves against civil disobedience. In this respect, the contrast with the non-cooperation days was striking: From March 1919 until Febuary 1922, the Muslim community in Bombay was in the forefront of various anti-government campaigns. But those days had gone, and now the Viceroy could report with relief that:

> It is one of the most important features of the situation that the Muhammadans of Bombay as a community have kept aloof from the movement.[47]

Likewise, UP Muslims, once drawn into the national movement after the First World War, developed a sharp antagonism towards the Congress within a decade or so.[48] In the process, unity between Hindus and Muslims waned, their friendship and cooperation being replaced by communal bickering and violence. As a result, only a few Muslims joined civil disobedience.[49] Those who went to goal

Table Conference'. Sykes to Irwin, 30 January 1930, 25 August 1930, Sykes Papers (2-B). For further evidence, see Brown, *Gandhi and Civil Disobedience*, p. 137.

45 Ravinder Kumar, 'From Swaraj to Purna Swaraj', D.A. Low (ed.)' *Congress and the Raj* (London, 1977), p. 97.

46 AICC Papers (1/2), 1932.

47 Irwin to Wedgwood Benn, 24 April 1931, Irwin Papers (6). Also, references to Muslim opposition to civil disobedience in Bombay can be found in: Bulletin No. 3,16 January 1930, Hawkins Papers; Sykes to Irwin, 16 April 1930, Sykes Papers (2-A).

48 Gyanendra Pandey, *The Ascendancy of the Congress in Uttar Pradesh 1926-34: A Study in Imperfect Mobilization* (Delhi, 1978), p. 148.

49 In UP Muslim hostility was clear even in those areas which had generated wide support for non-cooperation in 1920-21. In Rae Bareli, for instance, Muslim opposition rested 'not so much on any inherent regard or

during 1930-33 were mostly men like T.A.K. Sherwani, Rafi Ahmad Kidwai and Manzar Ali Sokhta, Congress leaders in their own right and usually men who had close links with the Nehrus.[50] But the Nationalist Muslims, in general, were reluctant participants.[51] Ansari, for instance, joined civil disobedience partly due to the persuasion of Azad[52] and partly because he felt that, as a disciplined soldier, he should not refuse the marching orders of his officer.[53]

affection for government, or upon absence of national feeling, as upon distrust and suspicion of the Hindu Community, and the fear of being swamped by them'. A.P. Hume to G.K. Darling, 4 May 1332, Hume Papers (II-A), South Asian Archives, Centre for South Asian Studies, Cambridge.

50 Pandey, *op. cit.*, p. 112.

51 Khaliquzzaman, for example, wrote: 'As for Mahatmaji's civil disobedience programme, to tell you the truth, I have not been able to understand it much less appreciate it. . . . Mahatmaji is sadly optimistic and we shall have to reap its consequences'. Khaliquzzaman to Ansari, 1 March 1930, Hasan (ed.), *Muslims and the Congress*, pp. 111-112.
Subsequently, Khaliquzzaman was persuaded by Ansari to accept the 'dictatorship' of the banned national Congress; he wore the 'crown' uneasily for three months. Khaliquzzaman, *Pathway to Pakistan*, quoted in Pandey, *op. cit.*, p. 145.

52 Abul Kalam Azad, *India Wins Freedom: An Autobiographical Narrative* (Bombay, 1959), p. 11.

53 It may be noted, however, that Ansari was totally opposed to the Congress decision to launch civil disobedience, and tried to induce the working committee (CWC) to defer starting civil disobedience. But having failed in his efforts, he resigned from the membership of the Delhi Congress Provincial Committee, and refused the general secretaryship and membership of the CWC. In a statement, he said:

> . . . . my contentions were that the Congress should have fully utilised the peace offer made by the Viceroy; that it should not have closed the door against further negotiations by changing the Congress creed and that it should not have declared war by calling the country to launch upon a campaign of mass civil disobedience. Further it should not have shelved the solution of the minority question. My reasons for holding these views were that we were not ready for a countrywide mass movement of this nature; that there were great chances of the non-violent campaign being submerged by breaking out of violence and lastly, that the only sanction nccessary for the success of a non-violent campaign, i.e., Hindu-Muslim-Sikh unity, was wanting.

However, Ansari hastened to add that he neither considered the policy and programme of the Congress entirely 'ill conceived and detrimental to the larger interests of the country', nor did he believe that the civil

But this was small consolation to the Congress which appeared particularly sensitive to the charge that civil disobedience was a purely Hindu affair. At the same time, it could hardly deny increasing evidence of Muslim neutrality or hostility towards civil disobedience.

disobedience campaign was 'conceived in a spirit of antagonism to the Muslims'. Quoted in Hasan (ed.), *Muslims and the Congress*, p. 115; Ansari to the Raja of Mahmudabad, 11 April 1930, *Ibid.*, p. 121.

6

AN ASSESSMENT

It is hard to assess the role of a mind which drifted from smart triviality to adoloscent day-dreaming and back again. Apart from a supreme gift of expression, Mohamed Ali did not voice any great principle or order which were to guide his political activities. Power was too practical an affair to interest him. He relished the trappings of power, not the reality—the drama of great debates, the high-sounding titles, his name echoing through history. He was too outspoken to be a good manager of men and could never be a successful leader of any political party. He excelled at exposing the follies of others, but had little to advocate himself; his own thinking was ruthless—he spared nothing and nobody. Hinting at Mohamed Ali's inability to get on with others, Jawaharlal Nehru observed: 'Mohamed Ali had a nimble wit, but sometimes his devastating sarcasm hurt, and he lost many friends thereby'.[2] Abbas Tyabji,

1 Abdul Haq offered an assessment of Mohamed Ali in the following words:

> Though Mohamed Ali was a brilliant writer, essayist and an excellent orator, he lacked balance and a sense of proportion in his writings and speeches. He was a champion of freedom and independence, but he would have been ruthless and authoritarian in authority. . . . He often lost his temper at the slightest pretext, and had no consideration for friends and their loyalty to him. As a result, he alienated his friends and colleagues. . . He launched several ventures in great style, but was temperamentally incapable of carrying them to their logical culmination. . . . It is a pity that Mohamed Ali had no control over himself, a weakness which contributed to his failures. . .

Abdul Haq, *Chand Hum A'asr*, p. 164.

2 Nehru, *An Autobiography*, p. 117.

president of the Gujarat Conference which voted for non-cooperation before the Calcutta Congress (September 1920), wrote to Gandhi in October 1920:

> Whatever opinion you and the Khilafat Committee may have of the Ali Brothers many of us take them to be splendid agitators and very little more. They certainly are not the type of men in whom we would have much faith, were they placed to rule over us.[3]

Mohamed Ali was a passionate man, strong in his resentments as in his affections. He left a strong although not wholly pleasant impression on all who knew him;[4] of a man devoted to his convictions, resolute, self-confident, courageous and sincere. At the same time, he was obstinate, impatient in temper, and choleric in disposition; quick to anger when honour or religion was touched, wild and untameable; in W. Blunt's description of Jamaluddin Afghani, 'a wild man of genius'. Indeed, he wasted years of his life trying to make a hero out of the Turkish Sultan—as perverse a task as was ever attempted—and was determined to use any weapon which would restore the temporal glory and security of the Turkish Empire. He was neither influenced by the Turkish revolution, organised during the turbulent decade of Young Turkish

3 Quoted in Brown, *Gandhi's Rise to Power*, p. 276. This opinion was shared by many of Mohamed Ali's contemporaries. One of them wrote to Tej Bahadur Sapru: 'Frankly, I am not very much interested in the Ali Brothers. I do not believe in them, and to the extent that they are doing right, it is because they are either attracted by Gandhi's glamour, or they feel that they can work more effectively under the kudos of his name'. S.L. Polak to Sapru, 8 July 1981, Sapru Papers, vol. 17, p. 241, National Library, Calcutta.
Equally interesting is the impression of Percival Spear who met Mohamed Ali in St. Stephen's College, Delhi, in 1924. He writes: 'He was a handsome bearded man with striking eyes and clothed in flowing robes. His speech was easy, his manner ingratiating, that of a willing sufferer for a noble cause. To me he seemed to be too suauve to be sincere and too insincere to be noble. In fact I took an instant dislike to him'. Percival and Margaret Spear, *India Remembered*, (Delhi, 1981), p. 15.

4 After his meeting with Mohamed Ali, Edwin Montagu noted: 'Mohamed Ali is a quite typical specimen, full of incurable vanity'. Montagu to Chelmsford, 23 June 1920, Chelmsford Papers, MSS.EUR.E. 264 (6) IOL.

rule (1908-18) and so forcefully directed against the tyrannical rule of the Sultan as against western imperialism, nor by the views of men like Ziya Golp, the intellectual leader of that period, who dismissed the idea of uniting all Muslim nations under one ruler as merely a messianic hope.[5] In fact while Mohamed Ali and the Khilafatists were striving to recreate the Khilafat of the classical theorists, Muslims in other countries were busy establishing national states independent of external ties of domination.

Mohamed Ali's reputation rested on his passionate, vocal, and forceful advocacy of what came to be identified as the religio-political interests of the Indian Muslims. Though his early journalistic ventures were supported by the Raja of Mahmudabad and Nawab Hamidullah Khan of Bhopal and, towards the end of his life, he drifted into the camp of the Muslim landlords, he was not the spokesman of a class. In this respect, Mohamed Ali was different from many of his comrades who sought political power in order to bolster their social status and to advance their personal, sectional, or class ends. In his case, politics was a means to achieve higher social and religious ideals, defined by the Quran and reflected in the life of the Prophet Mohammad, the promotion of the concept of Muslim brotherhood and the protection of Islamic institutions everywhere. These ideals could hardly be accomplished within the narrow framework of institutional politics; so Mohamed Ali scrupulously avoided taking part in the politics of legislative councils, district boards, and municipalites. His interest in the political demands of the Muslim League was peripheral; so was his involvement in the debates over communal electorates and communal representation. The only occasion when he spoke and wrote on these issues with some seriousness was during the Nehru Report controversy. But his interest was not sustained for long; he reverted to his favourite theme of 'Muslim unity' and pan-Islamism at the Round Table Conference. He expressed the dilemnas and the anguish for those Indian Muslims who were torn between their passionate desire to see their homeland free and their desire to serve their Islamic faith and their special interest in political life.[6]

In Mohamed Ali's view, there was just one world of Islam, one

5 See Uried Heyde, *Foundations of Turkish Nationalism: The Life and Teachings of Ziya Golp* (London, 1950), pp. 92-3, 101.

6 Hardy, *Partners in Freedom*, p. 47.

vast brotherhood stretching across the world.[7] This was best summed up in the *Comrade* of 18 January 1916.

> It is not only one God, one Prophet and one Ka'aba that the Muslims of the world have in common, but in every degree of longitude and latitude they hold the same views of the relations of husband and wife, of parent and child, of master and slave and of neighbour and neighbour ......They follow among all races the same laws of marriage, divorce and succession. And they do this in the twentieth century of the Christian era exactly as they did in the sixth and hope to do so to the last syllable of recorded time. . . there is still the one God to worship and the one Prophet to follow, and through calm or storm there is always one unaltered and unalterable Book to soothe and to stimulate, and the one Ka'aba to act as the magnetic pole for all true Believers from all points of the compass.

Such a vigorous assertion of the unity of all Muslims, inspired by the pan-Islamic notions of Jamaluddin Afghani, ignored the divisions which set Muslims apart at all levels. Emphasising the primacy of religious loyalty and the unifying role of Islamic tradition and symbols, Mohamed Ali evolved a framework which relegated caste, class, linguistic and regional identifications into the background, and sought to project the image of a monolithic Muslim community. For this reason he was not only preoccupied with issues of a religious nature—the Kanpur mosque affair, the Khilafat question, and the Sarda Marriage Bill[8]—but also made repeated

7 Askari 'Mohamed Ali: Ek Sada-i-Shikast Sa'az', *Aligarh Magazine*, 1960-61, p. 109.

8 The Hindu Child Marriage Bill was introduced by Harbilas Sarda in the Legislative Assembly in February 1927. The Bill, which sought to fix the lowest limits for the age of consent for boys and girls at 18 and 14 respectively, was passed in 1929. The Muslims, however, insisted on being excluded from the operation of the Act, threatening that they would be roused into open revolt, because the Act penalized early marriages while the *Sharia* had left early and late marriage a matter of choice. A statement presented to the Viceroy on 9 November 1929 on the issue was probably drafted by Mohamed Ali. He was also in correspondence with many influential Muslims in an attempt to organise a crusade against the Sarda Act. See Iqbal (ed.), *Writings and Speeches*, p. 438; K.A. Siddiqi to

pronouncements about his unswerving loyalty to Islam. Mohamed Ali argued that the Muslims have had a pre-eminent sense of community in their *Weltanschaung*, and especially so in India, where their adherence to Islam made them unique and gave them their 'communal consciousness'. 'I have a culture, a polity, an outlook on life—a complete synthesis which is Islam', he said at the Round Table Conference. He added:

> Where God commands I am a Muslim first, a Muslim second, a Muslim last, and nothing but a Muslim. If you ask me to enter into your Empire or into your nation by leaving that synthesis, that polity, that culture, that ethics, I will not do it.[9]

He did not, however, believe that by being a Muslim he was any less an Indian. His religious beliefs and nationality never appeared to him to be incompatible. He could—and must—be true to both Islam and India. In an interview to the *Independent* of Allahabad, he stated his political creed in the following words:

> I am a Muslim first and everything else afterwards . . . As a Muslim, I must be free and subject to no autocrat who demand from me obedience to his orders in defence of those of God . . . Faith is my motive of conduct in every act . . . . and my faith demands freedom. That Swaraj will give me, but it does not demand the subjugation of the Hindu or any one else differing from me in faith . . . My own freedom and not the enslavement of any other is my creed.[10]

In order to prove the compatibility of his loyalty to Islam and to his country, he took great pains to explain that 'where India is concerned, where India's freedom is concerned, where the welfare of India is concerned, I am an Indian first, an Indian second, an Indian last, and nothing but an Indian'.

Mohamed Ali, 2 January 1930, MAP. Mohamed Ali's opposition to a progressive legislation was a retrogressive step. It is, however, interesting to note that his biographers have conveniently ignored his attitude towards the Sarda Act in an attempt to sustain the enlightened image of Mohamed Ali.

9 Iqbal (ed.), *Writings and Speeches*, p. 405.

10 *Mussalman*, 13 May 1921.

It is interesting to note that Mohamed Ali's view of the Indian Muslim community took no account of its regional diversity; hence his inability to appreciate the aspirations of the more vocal Bengali and Punjabi Muslims.[11] For instance, he was unable to understand why many Muslims of these provinces were reluctant to join his crusade against the recommendations of the Nehru Report. Their intransigence was a frustrating experience for one who had raised the banner of 'Muslim unity' so consistently. Indeed, after this experience he considered it necessary to reaffirm his belief in the 'unity' of all Muslims, cemented by the ties of religion. He chose the plenary session of the Round Table Conference to do so, harping on his familiar theme before a predominantly British audience. He sustained his image of an iconoclast and a visionary, but seemed surprisingly unaware of the complexities of the problems he dealt with in his address.

II

Some historians are disposed to overlook or minimize Mohamed Ali's contribution to the heightening of Muslim communal consciousness; indeed they tend to magnify the importance, and the consistency of his political role.[12] It is conveniently ignored that, at least during the Khilafat ferment, Mohamed Ali was at the centre of many controversies, the source of discord within the ranks of the Khilafatist, and the initiator of several ill-conceived projects. His invitation to the Amir of Afghanistan (2 April 1921) to liberate India from British imperialism was indiscreet,[13] and his occasional outbursts at the Khilafat Conferences exacerbated existing tensions between the Khilafatist and their Congress supporters.[14] So was the

11 This is clearly borne out in Mohamed Ali's articles on Iqbal, published in *Hamdard*. See Atiq Siddiqi, *Iqbal: Jadugar-i-Hindi Nizad* (Delhi, 1980).

12 This refers, in particular, to the works of Qureshi and Shan Muhammad.

13 Mohamed Ali's view was endorsed by Azad who stated that 'whatever Mohamed Ali said was quite compatible with the teaching of Islam'. Home Poll. 1921, 45, NAI. Later, of course, Mohamed Ali offered a clarification to remove the misunderstanding in the minds of the Hindus. See his Presidential Address at the Allahabad District Conference in May 1921, Home Poll. 1921, 10, NAI.

14 For example, the Urdu poet Brij Narain 'Chakbast' expressed his apprehensions in response to Mohamed Ali's speech at a Khilafat Conference in April 1921. He wrote: 'Mohamed Ali's speech has convinced me that

idea of the ill-fated *Hijrat* to Afghanistan, the so-called *dar al-Islam*; it revealed serious limitations in the vision and perspective of a man who claimed to shape his community's destiny. The *fatwa* on *hijrat*, issued by Abul Kalam Azad and endorsed by Abdul Bari of Firangi Mahal, illustrate the growing religious frenzy which guided the decisions of the chief architects of the Khilafat movement in India. Men like Mohamed Ali were swept by this religious frenzy, suspending their independent judgement and the will to exercise restraint on the activities of some Khilafat enthusiasts.

The *Hijrat* fiasco, the scandal over the 'misuse' of Khilafat Funds, and the petering out of the Khilafat euphoria after 1922 considerably damaged the reputation of many Muslim leaders, including Mohamed Ali. There was no longer any enthusiasm for his fanciful projects—for his grand design of uniting the *millat-i-Islamia* under the green flag. The *Comrade*, once financed through generous subscriptions, went bankrupt; it was closed down in January 1926.[15] The Ali Brothers, who always spent more than their limited means, found themselves in dire financial straits. 'Poverty is pestering me', Mohamed wrote to Shaukat and considered

the purpose of this political turmoil is to strengthen Islam and to create conditions in India which would provide Afghanistan with an opportunity to invade the country. I do not think that Muslims can be converted to Indian Nationalism because of their extra-territorial loyalty. Those who have read Mohamed Ali in the *Comrade* would realize that he is a Pan-Islamist by conviction; he is not a friend of the Hindus. . . . In fact, the study of Muslim political movements reveal their lack of trust in the Hindus. . . . Gandhi believed that the support of the Ali Brothers would enable him to promote his objectives. But, in effect, Gandhi has been used by the Ali Brothers as their instrument. Chakbast to Sapru, 28 April 1921 (in Urdu), Sapru Papers. In an 'Open letter to the Maulana Sahebs', the editor of *Bharatwasi*, conveyed his decision to oppose the Khilafatists because of their violent outbursts and because they designated themselves as 'Khadim-i-Ka'aba' and not as 'Khadim-i-Hind'. 'I ask you gentlemen', he wrote, 'whether in the circumstances it is possible for you to join hands with the Swarajists of India. I am from among those Indians who consider the attainment of Swarajya as their only *Dharma*, but for you the Swarajya for India is not the first duty. You build the whole edifice on religion, while we build the entire edifice on patriotic considerations of Swarajya. Do you think it is possible, in the circumstances, for both the parties to join hands?' P. Parasram to the Ali Brothers, 8 July 1921, MAP.

15 Shan Muhammad, *The Ali Brothers*, p. 248.

restarting the *Comrade* 'and see if I can wipe off the deficit due to those two journals or I shall retire from public life, and earn Rs. 50 from tuitions'.[16] The Raja of Alwar came to the rescue of the ailing Mohamed Ali and bore the expenses of his travel to and treatment in London.

Mohamed Ali's influence also began to wane in the aftermath of civil disobedience. The Congress politicians were wary of placing confidence in 'a nationalist in the winter season and a communalist in summer',[17] while his erstwhile Muslim followers had few reasons to be inspired by his leadership. Spurned by the Congress and ignored by his community, Mohamed Ali eventually clung to the much-maligned Khilafat Committees.[18] Before the news of the abolition of the Khilafat was stale, he tried to influence the Muslim League to pursue Khilafatist activities through negotiations with Ibn Saud. But he was voted down because the King of Hijaz, having demolished numerous sepulchers held sacred by Muslims, was generally unpopular because of his 'profanity'.[19] In fact, Mohamed Ali's unabashed defence of Ibn Saud alienated him from his spiritual mentor, Abdul Bari, from his fellow prisoners in his last incarceration—Maulanas Nisar Ahmad and Abdul Majid—and from his community which was incensed by the religious insensitivity of Ibn Saud and his territorial aggrandizement.[20]

In June 1926, however, Mohamed Ali discovered, much to his disappointment, that Ibn Saud had no sympathy with the religious concerns of his co-religionists.[21] He was also depressed by the squalor of the Holy Cities—Mecca and Medina—the barrenness of the surrounding land, the degeneracy of the social conditions, and the mismanagement of the *Haj* traffic.[22] So, on his return

16 *Searchlight*, 17 April 1927.

17 *Forward*, 14 May 1927. In fact, one of his former colleagues, Arif Husain Hasvi, resigned his post from the *Hamdard* because of Mohamed Ali's communal posture. *Ibid.*, 14 May 1926.

18 For example, Choudhury Khaliquzzaman, *Pathway to Pakistan* (Lahore, 1961), p. 69.

19 Hamid, *Muslim Separatism*, p. 186; Iqbal, *Life and Times*, p. 230.

20 They organised the *Khuddam-ul-Harmain* along with Hasrat Mohani and M.H. Kidwai. Qureshi, *Ulema in Politics*, p. 291.

21 In response to pressure from Indian Muslims, Ibn Saud convened a conference to which a deputation, under the leadership of Maulana Syed Sulaiman Nadwi, was sent by the Khilafat Committee.

22 Watson, *op. cit.*, p. 87, Qureshi, *Ulema in Politics*, p. 291.

to India from Mecca, he wrote an article complaining of the un-Islamicness of the Arabs. He was not, however, hopeless about the situation. He assured his readers that the Khilafat organization was working to bring about a truly Islamic rule in the Holy Land, and he outlined what the Indian Muslims should do; first of all, they should form a party around the nucleus of Khilafat group. They should attempt to persuade other Islamic peoples to their way of thinking, and thus achieve a united Muslim voice. They should contribute money, time, technical assistance, moral support to the Hijaz, and should make religious visits. Above all, they should devote themselves wholeheartedly to the reformation of the Centre of Islam, and thus earn the good requital in both worlds. Mohamed Ali was confident that the Muslims would not tolerate Ibn Saud's arrogation of control of the Holy Land, but if necessary would prove to him that they were determined to reestablish a genuine Islamic rule.[23]

With his boundless enthusiasm, Mohamed Ali continued to preach the gospel of pan-Islamism, though his community was unmistakably indifferent to his ideas and was particularly opposed to the revival of the Khilafat Committees. Among the former Khilafat leaders, Ansari, Azad, Ajmal Khan and M.H. Kidwai were not only reconciled to the abolition of the Khilafat, but decided to take an active part in the Congress movement and foster Hindu-Muslim unity. The Khilafat Committees, in their opinion, had lost their *raison d'etre* not only because the institution of Khilafat was abolished but also because they served to heighten communal consciousness and encourage Hindu-Muslim strife. Such was the view of Ansari who, after having conceded that 'pan-Islamism that was once an ideal is now a vague grievance; what was once a hope and inspiration is now a sorrow',[24] resigned from the communally-oriented Khilafat Committees. 'As an Indian owing allegiance first to the motherland', he wrote in July 1926, 'I feel I must sever my connections with all communal or sectional political organisations'.[25] Expressing his anguish and disillusionment

23 Watson, *op. cit.*, p. 88-89.

24 Introduction to Halide Edib, *The Conflict of East and West in Turkey* (Delhi, 1935).

25 Ansari to Shaukat Ali, 16 July 1926, Hasan (ed.), *Muslims and the Congress* p. 19.

with the Khilafat leaders, Ansari wrote to Shaukat Ali:

> After seeing how partisan spirit had utterly blinded you and how under its influence you had acted unfairly, and in a manner I could never have dreamt you capable of acting, my faith in your righteousness and fair play completely broke down. . . .I had been a loyal co-worker of yours for the last 18 years, who had idolised you, worshipped the very ground on which you trod. . .I had placed myself, and all that I had, ungrudgingly at your service but when I saw the clay feet of my idol I felt as if the world had turned topsy-turvy and that I could never, in future, trust any one whoever it might be. I suffered from mental nausea from which I have not quite got over and which I do not think I would ever be able to completely shake off. Such a complete mental change has come over me that I do not think I shall ever be the same man that I was before.[26]

Equally important was the attitude of Iqbal. He had regarded the Khilafat movement, which gave so much fervour to the Indian Muslims and united them for a short time with the Hindus, as a means for strengthening the cause of Islam; it unfolded later on aspects in which 'no sincere Muslim could join for a single minute'.[27] Instead of launching a tirade against Mustafa Kamal Pasha and his policies, as was the case with Mohamed Ali, Iqbal viewed his experiments sympathetically. Turkey, in his opinion, was the first Muslim country to shake off the fetters of medieval mentality and had found a way of life of her own.[28]

Such views, which gained widespread support amongst many western-educated Muslims, failed to impress Mohamed Ali. The Khilafat symbol was dead, but not so for the Maulana who refused to face the fact that Muslims themselves had played the final part in destroying what he and his comrades had been fighting to maintain. With a strange quixotic tenacity he continued charging

26 Ansari to Shaukat Ali, 14 May 1929, Hasan (ed.), *Muslims and the Congress*, pp. 64-65.

27 S. Nazir Niazi (ed.), *Maktubat-i-Iqbal*, vol. I, p. 158, quoted in Annemarie Schimmel, *Gabriel's Wings: A Study into the Religious Ideas of Sir Muhammad Iqbal* (Leiden, 1963), p. 47.

28 *Ibid.*, p. 48.

at the windmill, hugging an illusion which had already become irrelevant, and failing to objectively judge his position and activities in relation to the vicissitudes of historical development. He was not able to build the bridges for retreat because such skills did not fall in his sphere.[29] In the words of an admirer, Mohamed Ali

> was not a man to accept facts as facts. He was a born revolutionary aiming to destroy all that did not conform to his ideal, even though he might not be able to reconstruct what he had destroyed.[30]

29 Iqbal, *Life and Times*, see chapter fourteen.
30 Khaliquzzaman, *Pathway to Pakistan*, p. 69.

APPENDICES

1. To Mahfuz Ali*

Navsari
14 January 1910

Dear brother,[1]

You are mistaken in thinking that I was content with sending you a telegram of condolence. In spite of my best efforts, I failed to trace your whereabouts. Otherwise, how was it possible that having been in Rampur in August and November I would not have gone to Budaun to meet you ?

Your letter was heart-rendering and Bedil[2] and I wept for you. May God give you the strength to bear the loss !

After you left, the Council unanimously decided that I was in no way responsible for the decline in the cultivation of optum. Then, I applied for promotion which has been denied to me for so long. In the meantime, Mr. Dutt recommended against my promotion. About this time, some of my articles were published in the *Times of India* supporting the rights of Muslims and exposing the anti-Muslim role of Mr. Gokhale. Mr. Dutt was angry and asked for my explanation. I sent in a reply which was placed before the Council. In response, a general confidential circular was issued to government servants. They were told not to contribute articles which were likely to create communal animosity between different communities.

*(In Urdu), *Khutut-i-Mohamed Ali*, pp. 252-54.

1 Syed Mahfuz Ali (1870-1943) was born in Budaun and educated at the M.A.O. College. He served in the State of Khairpur (Sind) as assistant judge; resigned in 1901. In 1904 he was appointed a judge in Somaliland (Africa) on the recommendation of Theodore Morison.

2 Syed Hashim Husain belonged to Shahjahanpur. He was a close friend of Mohamed Ali and was associated with the *Hamdard*.

Sir Dunlop Smith and Sir Harold Stuart are trying their best to secure an appointment for me, and I hope that their effort will bear fruit.[3]

I have been transferred to the revenue department but I have been asked to serve as *Tehsildar* for six months before assuming change of *Naib-Subedar* in the district. I have been here for a month, but I hope to be informed of the government's decision soon. Sir Harold Stuart is trying to provide me with a job in the Secretariat; hopefully, my wishes will soon be fulfilled.

I can sit idle, but it is not possible for me to do so. I am fed up with this state. In fact, I am tired of this job.

I will leave this place on the 20th and reach Rampur on the 10th of Muharram. I will, then, attend the annual session of the Muslim League to be held in Delhi on 27-31 January. It would be nice if you could accompany me to Delhi.

I am a candidate of the old Boys' for the Board of Trustees. I hope you will get over your domestic grief and interest yourself in the affairs of the community. You will have to come for the Old Boys' dinner in March.

Your younger brother,
Mohamed

3 Mohamed Ali's hopes were not fulfilled. Dunlop Smith wrote: 'I have also heard from Bombay that there is no intention of appointing an Indian as Assistant Private Secretary. So all my trouble in writing has been thrown away'. G.S. Clark, Governor of Bombay, wrote the same. The Home Member, Harold Stuart, informed Mohamed Ali that 'I fear the Assistant Directorship of Criminal Intelligence is booked. Your name has occurred to me once or twice in that connection but your want of experience of detective work is a bar. . . .' Dunlop Smith to Mohamed Ali, 30 October 1909 ; G.S. Clark to Mohamed Ali, 2 November 1909 ; Harold Stuart to Mohamed Ali, 10 December 1909, MAP.

2. To the Nawab of Jaora[1]

Rampur
23 November 1910

Your Highness,

Since I left Indore 10 days ago, I have most carefully considered every aspect of Your Highness' very kind offer, as well as the arrangements I had already made for my future for the next year at least, before I was called by Your Highness. Believe me, Sir, it gives me great pain to say that I do not see any way to accept so flattering an offer.[2]

Considering the relation of Rampur and Jaora and specially Your Highness' ever ready courtesy and kindness to myself personally, it is truly painful to me to arrive at this decision after long deliberation. But I trust Your Highness will nevertheless count me as one of your devoted well-wishers who would ever be ready to do all that lay in his power for Your Highness and Your State.

Whether you continue the present arrangements in your State or work with Secretaries, I hope that Your Highness' efforts for the improvement of your State will meet with full measure of success.

Believe me, Sir,

Yours devoted well-wisher,
Mohamed Ali

1 The Jaora State was situated in the Malwa Agency of Central India with a population of 84,202 in 1901. Its ruler, Iftikhar Ali Khan, succeeded his father Muhammad Khan in 1895 and bore the title of His Highness and *Fakhr-ud-daula* Nawab *Saulat Jang*.

2 Regarding his reluctance to accept the minister's post in Jaora, Mohamed Ali wrote: 'I had suspected that the unopened telegram must be from the Young Prince whose pressing offer was being forcibly backed by no less a person than Sir Michael O'Dwyer, and I wished to avoid temptation at the last moment. By this change I had to give up an assured if modest income, and the prospects of all future advance, and like a plunger stake all the money I could gather from any quarter practically on one throw of the die as an Editor-Proprietor and subsequently as that unholy but costly Trinity-an Editor-Proprietor cum Proprietor'. *My Life: A Fragment*, pp. 31-32.

3. To James DuBoulay*

109 Ripon Street
Calcutta
3 January 1912

Dear Sir James DuBoulay,

I enclose copy of a letter which I have ventured to address today to Mr. Lucas. I feel that matters of detail regarding current Indian politics should in the first instance be referred to the Governor-General-in-Council, but my excuse for a departure from the general rule is the predominant necessity of instant action. I, however, trust that even this will be endorsed by reason of my sending a copy of the letter for the information of H.E. the Viceroy.

I also trust that my letter and the articles referred to therein will be able to persuade His Excellency that if any relief is due to the Muslims of Bengal it should be announced without delay. I am conscious of the fact that Lord Hardinge would certainly not like that there should be a Muslim agitation on the subject of the announcement; but I submit that well-merited concessions wisely made at a suitable moment would prevent such an agitation far more effectively than the most strenuous efforts of the leaders of Muslim opinion.

May I request you to be good enough to lay this correspondence before the Viceroy and to beg His Excellency to let me have some assurance from His Excellency, *if possible for early publication.*

With kindest regards,

Yours sincerely,
Mohamed Ali

*Mohamed Ali Papers, JMI.

4. To F.H. Lucas*

Calcutta
3 January 1912

Dear Sir,

Although the Marquis of Crewe[1] was kind enough to grant me an interview a week ago[2] which lasted close upon an hour, I generally abstained from referring to details of current Indian politics, as I feel that such matters are of a more direct concern of the Government of India than of the Secretary of State. For this reason I confined my own remarks to the international situation of Muslims and to the misunderstanding that they are too conservative, and even reactionary, in Indian politics—a misunderstanding to which their inherited instinct of making allowances for the difficulties of practical administration and the predominating need of safeguarding the interests af their own minority before advancing more nationalist claims, exposed them.

But there is one matter about which subsequent reflection persuades me with increasing urgency that an exception should be made, and that we should request the Secretary of State to call for proposals from the Goverment of India, if not to formulate some himself for the consideration of the Governor-General-in-Council. That is the position of the Muslims of Bengal after the far-reaching and sudden changes announced at the Durbar of His Majesty the King-Emperor.

I would respectfully invite the attention of the Secretary of State to the last three issues of the *Comrade* (dated 16th, 23rd and 30th December 1911) and particularly the last, in which the substance as well as the procedure of the announcement is discussed.[3] I hope

*Mohamed Ali Papers, JMI.

1 1858-1945; born in London and educated at Cambridge; Lord-lieutenant of Ireland (1892-95); lord privy seal (1908. 192-15); secretary of state for the colonies (1908-10) and for India (1910-15); created marquis in 1911.

2 Mohamed Ali met the Secretary of State on 24 December 1911. He was told in advance that 'your desire to see him in a purely private capacity and not with a view to the publication of any statement or report in your own or any other journal'.

3 In three articles entitled 'The Announcement', the time, place and procedure for the transfer of capital and the carrying out of the annulment of the

that His Lordship has been receiving these issues of the paper as they come out, but to make the matter sure I am sending herewith a copy of each of those issues[4].

It will be superfluous to discuss here the position of the Muslims of Bengal, but I may add that while other interests have either wholly gained, or gained as well as lost, no attempt has been made in the published Despatches to show that the Muslims of Bengal gain anything from the proposals of the Government which was not already theirs, while on the contrary the obvious fact is admitted—though, I submit, not with adequate emphasis—that their second state will certainly be worse than the first.

This, I think, could not have been expected to be well received by the Muslims, and at any rate, it is now obvious that it has not been well received. I cannot conceive that the Secretary of State or the Government of India will be content with such a state of affairs, and hoping that proposals to balance the losses of the Muslims may soon be under their consideration, we have ventured to suggest some ourselves in paragraphs 9, 10 and 11 of the leading article in the *Comrade* of December last,[5] in order to indicate some of the more pressing Muslim requirements. These, we are glad to learn, have met with general approval among the people concerned.

partition of Bengal were criticised. According to the *Comrade* of 23 December, the partition was modified in order to facilitate the shift of the capital from Calcutta. 'In order to do this with as little opposition from Bengal as possible, they (government) discovered in the modification of the Partition the necessary sugar-coating for a bitter pill'. The *Comrade* of 30 December referred to the government's decision as a boon which the government of India have their in unaided judgement and with a full-throated laudation of their generosity conferred on the 'loyal and contented Mussalmans'.

4 In reply, Lucas wrote: 'I am to say that your letter and the article referred to therein will recieve His Lordship's careful consideration, but that His Lordship is not prepared to make any statement upon them for publication'. Lucas to Mohamed Ali, 5 January 1912, MAP.

5 The *Comrade* suggested various concessions and 'some security' for the Muslims of Bengal in the Provincial and Imperial Legislatures and for all government posts in the 'gift' of the Bengal government. 'All these concessions should be announced immediately . . . The government must have learnt from the agitation against the Partition that the longer the wrong, real or supposed, remains unredressed the more difficult becomes the redress . . . He who gives at once gives twice, and we trust the government will give at once'.

My object in writing this letter, however, is not so much to press our own remedies for the undoubted evils as to invite the attention of the Secretary of State to the last paragraph of this article strongly recommending that whatever relief is to be given to the Muslims, it should be given immediately, and that it should be announced by His Majesty before departure. It is impossible to disguise the fact that for obvious reasons Muslim feeling in India is far from normal today. I would, therefore, respectfully suggest that the presence of His Majesty in India at this juncture should be fully utilised to restore its equilibrium to that feeling, and to bind still more firmly the seventy million Muslims of India to the Throne and Person of His Majesty. In my humble judgement it would be an infinite pity if such a great opportunity is lost through any avoidable delay, even if the delay is caused by the need for greater deliberation.

I would request you, Sir, to place this letter and the accompanying copies of the *Comrade* before his lordship, and to let me know, if possible, for early publication, what the Secretary of State proposes to do.

A copy of this letter is being sent to the Viceroy for His Excellency's information.

Believe me.

Yours faithfully,
Mohamed Ali

5. To Mahfuz Ali

109 Ripon Street
Calcutta
29 April 1912

My dear Mahfuz,

Why are you silent once more ? The *Comrade* of the 27th must have told you that the enterprise of the Urdu Daily is launched.[1] But even the *Titanic* was not unsinkable, and the *Hamdard* will be hopelessly at sea without the Man at the wheel and that is yourself.[2] Since launching this I have begun to take a peculiarly selfish interest in the 'White Beard'. One more reason why I should 'pray for your long and prosperity' as the petitions have it.

Do let me know how your affairs stand. I am writing to Hashim[3]—a thing which I should have done more than a fortnight ago had I not been so distracted by Ghulam Husain's ill-health and the worry of issuing the legal Prospectus after consultation with the solicitors. I hope that would be all right.

I hear from a Syed Shaukat Dehalvi that if I press Abdul Haq may come.[4] I am writing to him also tonight. You *must* write also immediately on the receipt of this, pressing him to come out. With you and Abdul Haq what could we not do. Of course, God is above us all and without his assistance nothing is possible. Ask Abdul Haq to write to you frankly on what terms he would care to come. He will not perhaps be so frank with me.

*Mohamed Ali Papers, JMI.

1 The *Hamdard* was 'intended to educate the people whereas the *Comrade* had to be their spokesman as well, and to act as a medium between them and their rulers. . . .' *My Life: A Fragment*, p. 59.

2 Mahfuz Ali joined the *Hamdard* in October 1912 and was on its staff for two years. He returned to Budaun where he contributed articles to an Urdu monthly, *Naqeeb*.

3 Syed Hashmi Faridabadi joined the *Hamdard* as a sub-editor. While he was a student at M.A.O. College, Aligarh, he was associated with the paper from early July to mid-September 1912. He was also deputed to persuade Abdul Haq—employed in the Translation Department of the Home Secretary's office in Hyderabad—to join the editorial staff of the *Hamdard*. But Hashmi's mission was a failure because the Home Secretary, Akbar Hydari, would not allow Abdul Haq lo leave. Abdul Haq was eventually persuaded by Nawab Imadul Mulk Bilgrami to decline Mohamed Ali's offer.

4 Abdul Haq expressed his inability to join.

As for yourself, when can you definitely come here ? I hope to order the Press etc. within a week i.e., if I get even half the number of applications with proper deposit. It will be at Delhi in that case by the middle of June. The only delay is likely to be caused by the type from Beirut.[5] The idea is to be able to start it all by the 1st *or at the latest* by 15th of July. But unless you reach me at least six weeks before that it will not be possible to start. We have much to arrange and Abdur Rahman[6] leaves by the 10th May. I shall have no. . . .* than. Do write to me a long letter saying *exactly when* you can come.

Yours,
Mohamed

5 A Beirut firm delayed the despatch of the type, 'and when it arrived it was insufficient and badly assorted for the purposes of 'copy' in the Urdu language. A second supply was ordered and was again delayed so that the first issue of the *Hamdard* could not appear for some eight months after the scheduled time'. *My Life: A Fragment*, p. 57.

6 Abdur Rahman Siddiqi was a member of the Indian Medical Mission to Constantinople.

*Illegible.

6. To A.M. Khwaja*

Kucha-i-Chelan
Delhi
28 May 1912

Dear Majid,

A complete eight-page issue of the *Hamdard* will be printed from the 1st of June. You must contribute articles for publication in first few issues and continue to do so from time to time. I hope it will not be necessary to remind you time and again.

If you don't, I shall kill—no—*kiss* you.[1]

Yours ever,
Mohamed

*(In Urdu) Abdul Majid Khwaja Papers, M-4, NML.

1 This line is in English.

7. To Mahfuz Ali*

Dacca
19 August 1912

Dear brother,

I was about to send you a telegram when your letter arrived conveying the news of your inability to come by August. You seem to think that your presence will be required in Delhi rather than in Calcutta. But before I stress the importance of your being in Calcutta, let me write a few words about Maulana Abdul Halim Sharar[1] and other aspirants for jobs in *Hamdard*.

I would certainly be pleased to associate a man of Sharar's stature with the *Hamdard*, for I think highly of his literary works.[2] At the same time, it is hard to ignore the difference between him, Abdul Haq and other 'graduates'. Sharar will neither be able to translate in English nor write a criticism of comments and reviews published in English journals. For this reason, we cannot pay him the salary offered to Abdul Haq.

I cannot, however, understand why Abdul Haq mentioned his salary to Sharar. In fact, I had decided to offer Rs. 200 to Abdul Haq but did not say so to him. Now it is for you to clarify this misunderstanding with Sharar and offer Rs. 200 on my behalf. In view of his inadequate knowledge of English, we will need to employ a translator at the cost of Rs. 50. This means that the

* (In Urdu), *Khutut-i-Mohamed Ali*, pp. 264-67. This letter has been slightly paraphrased and condensed here in translation.

1 Abdul Halim Sharar (1860-1926) lived in Matiya Burj, Calcutta (1869-1879), with his father who had joined the exiled Nawab Wajid Ali Shah in 1856. He returned to Lucknow to study at the Firangi Mahal Seminary and joined the staff of *Awadh Akhbar* as Assistant editor. In 1882, he launched an Urdu magazine *Mahshar*—'Day of Judgement'—followed by *Dil Gudaz*—'Quickener of the Heart'. When Mohamed Ali launched the *Hamdard*, Abdul Haq and Mahfuz Ali persuaded Sharar to join the editorial staff. He did so in September 1912, but left after three months.

2 Sharar was a prolific writer, having published one hundred and two books. He is remembered as a pioneer of the modern Urdu novel, a historian of refreshingly wide horizons, and an essayist equipped with a profound knowledge of Arabic, Urdu and Persian literature and Islamic theology. See E.S. Harcourt, Fakhir Hussain (eds.), *Lucknow: The Last Phase of an Oriental Culture* (London, 1975).

size of our editorial staff will be more than that of any prestigious English daily.

I am not acquainted with Qazi Talamuz Husain. He is not a celebrity and there is no reason to invite him to join the *Hamdard.* Anyway, we shall talk about him when we meet.

After reading your letter, I have concluded that, in spite of being a Syed, you are extremely stubborn. You consider your litigation and family disputes as important as the controversy over *Bagh-i-Fidak*[3]. How can you possibly ignore my preoccupation? My work remains unfinished even though I work tirelessly. In addition, how can I single-handedly publish a new daily newspaper, organise a modern printing press and correspond with newspaper agents? Then, my diabetes has rendered me useless and the doctors have warned me against too much work.

So, if you have any consideration for me, proceed to Calcutta immediately. Put a stop to your litigation and I will compensate for the loss you are likely to suffer. Do bring your younger son; he will enjoy himself. Your other children are grown up and are quite capable of looking after themselves.

At present, Mujtaba Saheb is working in your place. But I cannot impose any further burden on him. The calligrapher, Syed Hashmi, has been expecting you for a week and sitting idle without you.

I was so busy in Calcutta that this letter remained unsigned; I am signing it here in Dacca.

Mohamed Ali

3 Refers to a dispute between Fatima, the only surviving daughter of the Prophet, and Abu Bakr over the ownership of an orchard.

8. To Private Secretary,* Viceroy of India

Delhi
1 November 1912

[Telegram]

Some Muslims are anxious to advance a loan to Turkey. I understand such action would not contravene His Majesty's declaration of neutrality. May I beg you to place this telegram before His Excellency the Viceroy and to ascertain if such action is in any way contrary to law of British policy. Indian Muslims gratefully recognise the great efforts made by England to prevent Balkan aggression and are convinced of her desire for the preservation of peace. An authoritative declaration that government will not oppose the loan will confirm their confidenee in the goodwill of England towards Turkey and such sympathy as is not inconsistent with neutrality. I beg you to kindly send the reply by express telegram to enable me to announce it in the Juma Masjid after Friday prayers, and publish in Saturday *Comrade*.[1]

*Hardinge Papers, vol. 83, CUL.

1 The Viceroy wrote: 'The advance of loan by Muslims to Turkey would not contravene His Majesty's declaration of neutrality'.

9. To Private Secretary,* Viceroy of India

1 November 1912

[Telegram]

Please convey my hearty thanks to His Excellency for the message of assurance regarding advance of a loan by Indian Muslims to Turkey. The message was read out to a large congregation in the Juma Musjid and elicited great enthusiasm and grateful recognition of government's sincere sympathy. Shams-ul-ulama Syed Ahmed Saheb, Imam of the Juma Musjid, invited the congregation to express the thanks of the Muslims of Delhi for this clear declaration by His Excellency, and the congregation authorises me to convey their respectful gratitude.

*Hardinge Papers, vol. 84, CUL.

10. To J.S. Meston*

19 February 1913

My dear Sir James,

Will you forgive me for not acknowledging your very kind letter of the 27th January earlier than this? The fact is I was at Bombay when the letter reached Delhi and on my return a week later I thought the best answer would be my compliance with your desire that I may take an off-day and go over to Lucknow to see your Honour.[1] Every day since my return I have been endeavouring to get that off-day and to let you know when I would be in Lucknow but hitherto I have failed and see no chance of success sufficiently definite to inform Your Honour.

I shall, however, try my best to run up to Aligarh when you are there and to confirm once more what I have said before as to my anxious desire to cooperate with you and every well-wisher of my country and community in working for their progress. I fear these times are somewhat abnormal and the least difference in point of view is likely to create misunderstanding. But I feel sure that you mean the same thing and I have every confidence that I can satisfy Your Honour that my humble contribution to the work before us is in no way detrimental to the best interests of Government, the country and the Muslim community.

With very kind regards,

Yours sincerely,
Mohamed Ali

*Mohamed Ali Papers, JMI.

1 Meetings between Mohamed Ali and the Lieutenant-Governor were quite frequent. In October 1912 they met in Rampur as evident from the following:

My dear Muhammad Ali,

I was very glad to receive your letter, and need not assure you what pleasure it will give me to see you in Rampur. There is much that I want to talk over with you; and even if time is limited I hope we shall be able to continue our conversation at more leisure in Lucknow.

With sincere thanks for the kind wishes contained in your letter, and with all best regards,

Yours very truly,

Meston to Mohamed Ali, 10 October 1912, MAP.

11. Statement*

Events of a great moment and of a far-reaching character vitally affecting the Muslims have been taking place in rapid succession during the last two or three years, both in India and abroad, and it appears to our friends, as it appears to ourselves also, that a right understanding of the Muslim point of view is absolutely necessary in the interest of the Government, no less than in the interest of the Muslims themselves. Our friends have therefore advised us, and we agree with them, that at the present juncture it is necessary for us to go to England, for the purpose of explaining the Indian Muslims' point of view, and the salient features of the true Muslim situation in India and abroad, to His Majesty's ministers, the members of Parliament and other influential men in Great Britain, as well as the British nation at large through the important organs of the Press and by other suitable means, and to convince them of the essential loyalty of the Muslim community to His Majesty's person and throne, and of the justice of the Muslim claims.

Two of our eminent co-religionists, Mr. Jinnah and Khwaja Kamaluddin, are already in England, and we look forward with hope to their hearty cooperation. Of course H.H. the Aga Khan is also in Europe and we are confident of obtaining every encouragement and assistance from him.

But the object of our journey is by no means sectarian or exclusively communal. We firmly believe that the progress and well-being of Muslims are bound up with the progress and well-being of the country in which they live. The present carries in the womb the hopes and fears common to every community in

Comrade, 13 September 1913.

1 The mission sailed for England on 6 September 1913. On 12 September, the Viceroy informed the Secretary of State about the 'self-imposed mission' led by Wazir Hasan, 'a man of no importance whatever', and Mohamed Ali, 'a mischievous agitator largely responsible for creating the present situation by provocative misrepresentation in his paper'. The Viceroy 'strongly recommended that no encouragement be given to them'. Viceroy to Secretary of State (Telegram), 12 September 1913, Crewe Papers, CUL. The Secretary of State agreed and communicated the same message to, among others, the editors of various British newspapers, See Crewe to Burnham and John S.L. Strachey, 28 September 1913, Crewe Papers.

India, and we shall be failing in our duty not only as Indians but as Muslims also, if we do not strive during our sojourn in England to convert our fears into hopes and to materialise the hopes which we share with all our fellow countrymen. Mr. Gokhale is also in England at the present moment, and we hope to secure his sympathy and cooperation.

This is the mission on which we are today setting out, as fully conscious of its necessity and beneficience as of the great responsibility of our position. But we are also full of hope and of confidence in the goodness of our cause and in the desire as well as the ability of the great British nation to do us justice.

Time has been a dominating consideration with us and our departure has perforce been almost precipate. In fact, we had even less than a week in which to make the arrangement for our journey and to reach Bombay, and under the circumstances it has not been possible for us to apprise our people of our intention. But nevertheless we are confident that our action will commed itself to them and that their trust will go with us. We earnestly beg them to remember us in their daily prayers.

God willing, we shall return to them full of success as we leave them full of hope and confidence.

Mohamed Ali
Wazir Hasan

12. To James LaTouche*

Belgrave Mansions
Grosvenor Garden, S.W.
4 November 1913

Dear Sir James LaTouche,

In the course of our conversations we have came to know that considerable misconception exists in the minds of the authorities here about the purpose of our visit to this country, and that because of this we have to face difficulties which we should very much like to avoid. To remove this misconception, we enclose a copy of the message which we left for our people when leaving India, and we believe it has been published in all important newspapers in India.

From this you will see that what prompted us to come here was a series of events which had been taking place in rapid succession during the last two or three years, both in India and abroad, and not merely the unfortunate and deplorable happenings at Kanpur. You will note that we were advised by our friends to go to England for the purpose of explaining the Indian Muslims' point of view and the salient features of the true Muslim situation in India and abroad, in the first instance to His Majesty's Ministers, and afterwards to members of Parliament and other influential men in Great Britain, and, in the last resort, to the British nation itself, through the important organs of the press, and by other suitable means. As we then stated, we were anxious to convince them of the essential loyalty of the Muslim community to His Majesty's person and throne and of the justice of the Muslim claims.

Had we come here only for arranging a settlement of the Kanpur affair,[1] it stands to reason that we would have left for India soon after the satisfactory solution found by the statesmanship and courage of Lord Hardinge.[2] At it is we are still here and only at the beginning of our work.

To give you some more details of that work we may mention that when we left India the following questions were agitating the

*Mohamed Ali Papers, JMI.

1 The reference is to the Kanpur mosque agitation.

2 The initiative taken by the Viceroy eventually led to a compromise in Kanpur. His attitude was in sharp contrast to that of the intransigent Meston.

public mind, and induced us to undertake a journey to England to assist, to the best of our power, in achieving a satisfactory solution. The fate of Adrianople was then hanging in the balance, and we feel sure that His Majesty's Government could not have been left unaware by the Government of India of the intensity of Muslim feelings in the country on the subject of the British attitude towards Turkey over this question. Nearer home was the fate of the Indian, and particularly the Muslim press, which gave rise to the most lively apprehensions, in view of the judgment of the Special Bench of the High Court of Calcutta on the one side and the repressive action of various local government on the other. In the next place, only recently the Muslims of India had met at Aligarh in the Foundation Committee of Muslim University,[3] and passed several resolutions of far-reaching importance. In this matter particularly the final decision lay not with the Government of India, but with the Secretary of State, between whom and the Government of India there was considerable difference of opinion as the fact of several despatches having been exchanged between the two indicated.[4] In addition to these questions were those relating to the extension of a system of Executive Council Government to such provinces of India as were still without Executive Councils, and the separation of judicial and executive functions.[5]

Considering the fact that the *London Times* had published a series of articles on the subject of the attitude of Indian Muslims towards government insinuating the growth of disloyalty and attributing to them ideas and demands of a preposterous character which never crossed the minds of any responsible Muslim and particularly as the new constitution of the All-India Muslim League had been subjected to a good deal of uniformed and unjust criticism, and its resolution regarding self-government suitable for India as an ideal had been distorted into a more or less immediate demand, we felt that a repudiation of all these charges and suggestions in the Muslim press and from Muslim platforms in India, which had not proved as effective as we had wished, should be supplemented

3 The meeting was held on 26-27 July 1913.

4 On this point, see Aparna Basu, *The Growth of Education and Politica Development in India, 1898-1920* (Delhi, 1974); Rahman, *From Consultation to Confrontation*; Robinson, *Separatism Among Indian Muslims*.

5 The sixth session of the Muslim League (March 1913) passed a resolution on this subject.

by a series of our personal interviews with the authorities in this country, and an emphatic and clear explanation of the real attitude of Indian Muslims towards government which we maintain is as loyal today as it has ever been in the history of our community.

We have already stated that in the first instance we desired to deal with the authorities concerned, and you will see that we have made it clear after our arrival that until and unless we are finally told that the authorities here will have nothing to do with us, we do not intend to give publicity to our views and opinions. In a meeting of the Positivist Society held at Essex Hall on the 26th October, which you will note was more than a month after our arrival in London, Mr. Mohamed Ali said that 'we have purposely avoided hitherto the publication of our views through important organs of the Press in order to give no chance to anyone in authority to accuse us of coming here to embarrass His Majesty's Government' Only yesterday Mr. Wazir Hasan has written to the *Times* a rejoinder to the very misleading article about the resignation of Mr. Ameer Ali and a projected dinner suggested by the Aga Khan which had appeared in the issue of that paper for 31 October, and in the course of that letter he says, 'we do not, however, desire to discuss these publicly before bringing them to the notice of the authorities responsible to His Majesty and to the British Parliament, and in the last resort to the British public for the good government of our country. For this very reason we have hitherto refrained from public agitation, and we feel that in the first instance our concern is with the Secretary of State for India and those who assist him in his work at the India Office'.

We hope the above is a sufficiently clear and convincing explanation of our position and the objects we had in view in coming to England, as also of the methods we desire to pursue here. We have only to add that we intended to leave England about the middle of November, but as we have not even had an interview with the Secretary of State for India, we have postponed our departure for a fortnight, and we trust that you will kindly convey to Lord Crewe our anxious desire to place the view of the Indian Muslims on the various questions which we have enumerated before His Lordship, should he kindly grant us an interview. The time at our disposal is now very short, and we trust His Lordship will favour us with an interview at the earliest date convenient to him.

We cannot conceive that His Lordship can be unaware of our representative character, for the Council of the All-India Muslim League and many other Provincial and District Leagues and Associations and large Muslim bodies throughout the country have passed resolutions accrediting us as their agents, and if we fail to get the ear of the authorities here, we do not exaggerate in saying that their disappointment will be very great, and nobody will regret more the feelings likely to be stirred by such disappointment than the best friends of the government and of the Indian Muslims.

Apologising for the length of this letter and hoping for an early and favourable answer.[6]

We remain,

Yours very truly,
Syed Wazir Hasan
Mohamed Ali

6 Touche replied on 11 November saying that 'this request of yours goes far beyond the range of the object of the interview that I believed you to desire, and it is not possible for me to comply with it'. Crewe Papers.

13. To G. Bernard Shaw*

26 November 1913

Dear Sir,

It may appear as needless flattery if I said that I am a great admirer of yours, and possibly even flattery coming from so humble as myself may savour of impertinence. However, it is a fact and the only explanation of my anxious desire to make acquaintance unless I add to this motive another of a somewhat more selfish nature, namely, the desire to interest you in the affairs of my country and my co-religionists. When I was witnessing the performance of you 'Androcles and the Lion' at the Vaudeville I realised how much of your criticism of life was applicable to the existing conditions of India, and particularly of Muslim India and the Islamic world in their relation to the British government, and it made me feel all the more keenly my old wish to induce you to make India and Islam themes of your critical studies of life. Unfortunately our stay in this country has been much too short to enable us to carry out all our wishes with respect to cultivating the acquaintance of notable people and particularly leaders of thought in Great Britain, and I was sorry that an engagement of yours deprived me of the pleasure and privilege of meeting you at the Cecil Dinner given by the Islamic society to us on the 11th instant. We are now leaving England on the 1st December but late as it seems to be, I am not yet hopeless of being able to see you, and I write ask if I could call between now and Monday next at any time that is conveninent to you.

I remain,

Yours faithfully
Mohamed Ali

*Crewe Papers.

14. To A.M. Khwaja*

Chhindwara
13 February 1916

My dear Khwaja,

I can understand your silence. That's the result of being 'too late' in organising your forces. Aftab and Co[1] have had the biggest success in the last Trustees' meeting, for the election of some ten or twelve reactionaries and young ones, too, means little chance of your getting a majority in that body for ages, unless the present constitution is changed which cannot be done without a Trustees' majority[2]. The only other remedy is a fight in the public and refusal to give a penny more to the Trustees from the University Fund income and other sources unless they reform the constitution. For this, you fellows don't seem to have the energy and spirit. So we shall go on 'fighting for the good', but always 'vailing at the evil'.

The University meeting comes off on the 10th April[3] and I suppose you think it is so far off that you can go to sleep for another couple of months. I see no sign of your waking up and tackling Aftab's fallacious but somewhat clever (tho' wholly unscrupulous) pamphlet. Nor can I find any sign of your asking Mahmudabad publicly what he has done since 26th July 1913 to carry out the mandate of the Foundation Committee. You will talk and do nothing. I am really despairing of you 'the educated Muslims'.

*A.M. Khwaja Papers, M-4, NML.

1 The group of Aftab Ahmad Khan and Co. included Mir Wilayat Husain, Shaikh Abdullah, Habibullah Khan, Syed Tufail Ahmad, and Aziz Ahmad Bilgrami.

2 This refers to the Board of Trustees, established in 1889, and dominated by Aftab Ahmad Khan and his friends in the first decade of the twentieth century. Mohamed Ali was the main critic of the board and, as early as 1904, he worte articles in the Lahore *Observer* attacking the older generation of trustees for surrendering power to the British.

3 The Muslim University Foundation Committee met to ratify the acceptance of a university on the terms offered by the government. It did so in spite of strong opposition from the friends of the Ali Brothers, including Abdul Majid Khwaja. In the words of Gail Minault and David Lelyveld, the decision to accept a university on government terms 'ended the plan for a grandiose, independent, central Muslim institution'.

You wake up only to shout at the end of a row when you have been tricked and beaten by the reactionaries. You expose the unscrupulousness of your opponents, but this is every one knows they are cheats. What then?

Shaukat wants me to hurry you up about the cards. Do not wait for the exhibition. The thing can be done in a week if you and Qayyum and one or two others buck up. Do let me know how many have been sold. Then we shall let you know where to send the money.

I want you to write to me what happened at the dinner given by Mahmudabad to Sir Sankaran Nair. Also what happened at the Trustees' meeting when my resolution came up for discussion.

And lastly, what you propose to do now. As for Shaikh Sahib's election[4], I will damn you if he gets elected . . .*

Yours ever,
Mohamed

4 This refers to Shaikh Abdullah, the distinguished pioneer in Muslim female education. He was allegedly assaulted by Shaukat Ali joint-secretary of the Old Boys' Association, at a meeting of the Muslim Educational Conference in 1905. In the scandal that followed, Shaukat Ali was forced to resign his position as a trustee.

*Illegible.

15. To Abdul Majid Daryabadi*

Chhindwara
25 July 1916

My dear Mr. Abdul Majid,

Yes, it was at my own desire, as you remind me, that your *Psychology of Leadership* was forwarded to me and I am indeed flattered by your remark that I am one of the very few persons whose opinion of the said book you cared to know and should have felt much interested in knowing. Well, even if I had not received a complimentary copy, I would have most probably written to you on the subject of the book. But then I read in the papers that immediately after your wedding you motored out to some place for your honeymoon, and I concluded that the 'psychology of love' would consider any reference to the 'psychology of leadership' as an unwarranted and ungenerous intrusion at least throughout the 'moon'. Hence the delay. I hope this plea will be acceptable.

Now I turn to the book. I welcome it as a book of serious thinking and an indication of wide reading no less than careful observation. Reading is as rare in our 'intellectuals' as thinking and even a careful study of the thoughts of others would have merited praise. But from the illustrations that you have given of different psychological phenomena, it is manifest that you have not been content with the thoughts of others. I can say much more in the same strain, but I understand that you do not desire an 'appreciation' only but want a critique. Had we been together I could have given my views, for what they are worth, in very much greater detail. But a letter has far too meagre propositions for a detailed criticism of a book on philosophy and you will have to be content merely with rough suggestive notes. They will be very disjointed and will, I am afraid, give you an idea of desultory and casual reading of the book. But, I assure you, I read slowly as a rule and, in this case particularly, I took several days to study the book thoroughly. Be that as it may, here are the rough, disjointed notes:

1. *Style.* I congratulate you on a very full acquaintance or rather familiarity with modern philosophical phraseology and

*Abdul Majid Daryabadi Papers, NML.

diction. It has the merit of clear definition and one who is intimate with the language of modern psychology is not likely to misunderstand your meaning. But, perhaps, you do not altogether ignore the fact that your book will find readers among the 'crowd' as well, and howsoever little you may care for the praise of the groundlings you cannot ignore their needs. And their need is a less technical diction or rather simpler explanation and greater illustration accompanying the diction of modern psychology. Perhaps I exaggerate this a little, as I am myself addicted to the vice of diffusiveness and am not content merely with suggestion, going too often into cramming things into the reader and not leaving much to do himself. But I think your book could well have been twice its size without being too diffusive.

2. *The Plan.* Here I find a disproportion in the detailed study of the 'crowd' and too much compression and rushing over when you come to the 'leaders' of the crowd. It is quite legitimate to discuss the psychology of the crowd and then make a negative study of its leaders by assigning to them a greater proportion of the qualities which the crowd as compared with its individual components lacks. But you must remember that if crowds can be treated with much generality, its leaders cannot, for they possess far greater individuality and personality. You cannot group them with the same care as you can group the crowds. When you revise this book, I would strongly recommend a change of 'scale', so to speak, in your treatment of leaders. This part of the book needs fuller treatment and much amplification is possible and even necessary.

3. *The 'Crowd'.* I agree with your main thesis about the crowds, but here too, a greater differentiation is needed. I note that you admit the great merit of discipline which 'crowds' may possess and which makes them a great dynamic force as useful as it is indispensable. But your idea of the 'crowd' appears to be more of 'mass meetings' and 'demonstration' such as we have in India only too often, and not have *trust* in the 'crowd' tampered by *caution*, not *mistrust*, tampered by *fear*, as he has.

4. *Leadership.* You rather give me an idea in your book that it is all a long sustained series of tricks and subterfuges, an endless gulling of silly people consciously undertaken and deliberately carried out—a sort of Maskelyn and cook jugglery—all illusion

and *maya*. Of course you don't say so. In fact, you occasionally differentiate between what you call true and false leadership. But, psychologically speaking, is there anything *true* or *false*? To psychology, all that *is* is true. But the motives of actions differ and morally some are condemnable while others are worthy of commendation. I expected you to discuss in detail the actions or rather the failings and thoughts of various kind of leaders, including those who consciously mislead and deceive and those who deceive themselves before they unconsciously deceive others and yet again those who unconsciously deceive others first and then end by deceiving themselves. This part of the book is rather hurried and too general and not sufficiently definite for a psychological study.

5. *Illustrations*. These, as I have said before, are in my humble opinion not ample enough. Besides, they are very unequal. The Nadwa incident of poor old Shibli[1] and the Calcutta rowdies treatment of a couple of Christian preachers do not deserve to be used as illustrations in a book in which you deal with so many historic incidents well-known to all or at least to most of your readers.

6. *Reference to the Prophet*. My last criticism is with reference to your use of the Prophet and the *Quran* for purposes of illustration. I regard you as a *True Believer* in its strictest sense and therefore astonished at the profanity, if I may term it, of your references to so sacred a personality and so sacred a scripture. Is it a laboured display of 'detachment' and 'stern secularity' or what? This, I ask, not as a critic concerned only with the psychology of leadership, but as a *Muslim* critic concerned also with the deference properly expected in a *Muslim* author towards the Messenger of God and God's own word. I am certainly glad that you have not

1 Shibli Nomani joined Aligarh College in 1883 as professor of Persian and assistant professor of Arabic. 'I was fortunate enough', recalled Mohamed Ali, to attend his all too brief lectures to the undergraduates on the Quran. . .'. In 1908, Shibli joined the *Nadvat-ul-ulama* as Principal but was forced to resign in July 1913. On 7 March 1914, the students went on strike ostensibly in connection with the expulsion of a student, but really, as would appear from the reasons given to the board of enquiry, because the students were prevented from attending the lectures of Shibli and from taking part in a meeting of the Kanpur mosque incident. For further details, see Syed Sulaiman Nadvi, *Hayat-i-Shibli*, pp. 652-654.

confined yourself to merely so-called secular leaders and have utilised the great figure of our glorious Prophet for illustrating leadership and its psychology. But your references only too often savour of the spirit of Christian missionaries who set out to prove, or at least subtly suggest in the minds of those who believe in him, that Mohammed (May I and my family sacrificed on the altar of his Faith) was (God forbid) a 'false prophet' and a 'charlatan'. Why are you even critical of the Quranic injunction against the rowdyism of the Qurayash and the Jews who used to flock the Prophet's discourses only to break up the meetings or talk him out or laugh him out? If you consult any ordinary *sira* you will find the splendid descension of the verses about speaking gently in the presence of the Prophet. Again, I fear you have allowed one of the most magnificient instances of great leadership to be wasted, (or rather misused) when quoting the words of the Prophet to Sa'd ibn-i-'Uhaid[2] when he voiced the complaint of the *Ansar*[3] about a disproportionate division of the booty among the *Muhajirins*[4]. Do you think that was jugglery and deceitfullness? I do hope you don't. But you certainly give the impression.

Speaking frankly about your treatment of leadership, I wish you had kept a discussion of the *technique* of leadership apart from a discussion of the *quality* of leadership. We are all somewhat theatrical in our public life. We all pose and attitudinize. That is why so few of us are heroes to their valets and still fewer to their wives. But no less than 40 years did our great Prophet spend in the midst of the Meccans as an ordinary man so that they could test his sincerity during his long apprenticeship. When after 40 years he had earned the title of 'the trusty' and had become a master in his sacred craft, God's word was first revealed to him. And how did he receive it? Why in pain, and fear and almost in doubt. And who came first to believe in him? The wife of his

*Traditional biography of the Prophet Mohammad.

2 He was a companion of the Prophet and an Ansar of great reputation. He carried the standard at the conquest of Mecca.

3 'the helpers', title of the believers of Medina who received and assisted the Prophet after his *hijrat* from Mecca.

4 'the emigrants', a name often applied in the Quran to those followers of the Prophet who had migrated from Mecca to Medina with him. The term *muhajir* is not applied to the Prophet himself.

bosom was the first. His boy cousin was the second. His dearest and closest friend was the third. Far from deceiving others who were outsiders before he could pose and attitudinize, he was himself relieved, and strengthened and confirmed in faith by those who saw him daily in the easy undress of homelife. This man, at least, was above trickery. It is true (that) God enjoined silence and gentle speech on all in his presence. But that was to establish 'prestige' such as a handful of foreign rulers may like to establish in order to govern millions. 'Prestige' in that sense (is) chagrin in the way of the admission of mistakes and blunders. But the Quran is full of exhortations addressed to the Prophet either just in time to save him from some blunder that he was about to commit or to guide him in future to avoid such an error as he had just committed. Any interpreter[5] will tell you that there is a special name for such indications of divine disagreement with the Prophet's actions or proposals. Again, a believer in 'Prestige' in that sense would have gloated over such an incident as the eclipse of the sun soon after the death of the Prophet's son which the superstitious Arabs believed to be the cause of the sudden darkness. But the *Quran* which had set out to destroy all superstitions took special care to destroy this one immediately . . . . .* But here out of the mouth of the Prophet himself God had the superstition spontaneously believed in discredited in its entirety. 'The sun and the moon suffer eclipses at their proper seasons and have nothing to do with the gasps or joys of men'. Then, again, his followers at least were willing, nay, anxious to believe that the Prophet's death would be the end of the universe. They could not help but believe that, and when he passed away, those whose faith was the greatest stood dumb and stunned with the shock. They had never thought of the possibility of an existence when the Prophet was no more. Those whose faith was weaker and those who were more superstitious than rationally believing were almost shocked out of their faith. Umar was himself so bewildered that, although like a great leader of men and a practical man he realized the need of something to restrain or comfort those men, he could devise nothing more than

5 In Islam the word *tafsir* means particularly the commentaries on the Quran and the science of interpreting the sacred book. The branch of learning—*ilm al-Quran wa'l-tafsir*—is a special and important branch of *hadith*.

*These lines are illegible but they most probably refer to certain superstitious beliefs regarding solar and lunar eclipses.

a threat to make a dead man of him who said the great Prophet was dead. At such a juncture it was the man whose faith deserved the title of '*muminun*' that pacified the people and reconciled them to the departure of the Prophet from this world. But how did he do it? Merely by quoting the verses which Mohammad (dearer to me than father, mother, wife or child) had himself proclaimed to the world. 'What is Mohammad but a Messenger. There have been other Messengers too before him. Should he die or be killed, will ye turn on your heels into infidelty'. Well, could Abu Bakr say that Umar was wrong; yes, Mohammad had died all of them must die; but the God of Mohammad was not dead. He was alive and eternally standing, for this was the life long sermon of the man who never permitted himself a dubious 'Benami transaction' so to speak. The doctrine of 'Prestige' as understood today demands for the agent of the administration something of the same sanctity and halo as sovereignty itself—something of a belief in the infallibility not only of law (which is *legally* and of necessity always *infallible*, for the king can do no wrong legally—there being no legal superior by whose standard he could be judged) but also by the administration of that law and in their, *obiter dicta* as well as in their judgements. This was to our Prophet paganism which he had been sent to drive out of the world. He was innocent or infallible only in as much as he was the Messenger of God and moral wrong or vice would have vitiated the Messenger and made his delivery of the Message a subject of doubt and hesitation. But he was anxious to confess that where he had no Law from the infallible Sovereign Lord of us all to promulgate, he was as fallible as any of his followers. In fact, 'you know best the affairs of your world' as he, a merchant of Mecca, told the agriculturists of Medina when their palm trees brought no fruits the year . . .

Well, I am afraid I have gone perhaps a little too fully into the matter and also because I may be only *wrongly* suspecting that you attribute conscious trickery to the sincerist leader of mankind. If so, forgive the digression or reconsider such passages in the book when it goes into a second edition, as I hope it will soon do. In the meantime accept my thanks for kindly presenting me with food for such thought.

With kindest regards,

Yours very truly,
Mohamed Ali

P.S. You suggest to me that I should write some book during my enforced leisure, and that our people expect one from me. If that is so, I am afraid they don't yet know me. Firstly, I have not the patient perserverance nor the temper of the researchist. Secondly, my emotions are much too strong to permit what intellect I may possess to be exerted in the writing of a book. As for my enforced leisure, no one would have allowed me to secure it had my emotions been so weak as to permit me to *write* history when others were *making* it. No, my friend, my brain is far too busy (and so is my heart) to allow of any leisure for such 'pas. times' as authorship. Occasionally the heart dictates a verse or two, to the brain and should you care for a *Ghazal* or two, I will send you some that I have been enabled to put on paper 'in the intervals of business', during what you will call the leisure of the last 15 months. A local . . . made the same suggestion as you have. I told him I could only write a volume on Karbala or 'Before the Hijrat' just now. A few of my verses will explain my meaning. Here they are:[6]

6 The verses have been omitted. They are, however, quoted in A.S. Shahjahanpuri (ed.), *Rais'ul Ahrar*.

16. To B.J. Tilak*

Chhindwara
12 November 1916

Dear Mr. Tilak,

This morning's paper brought the welcome news that the Bombay High Court has reversed the order of the District Magistrate of Poona demanding from you security 'to be of good behaviour' in consequence of the speeches you had recently delivered while inaugurating the Home Rule League.

As you are probably aware, the Censor of our correspondence is permitted not to pass any correspondence of a political character, so that even if I feel minded to do so I cannot deal with the political aspects of the High Court decisions nor with those of the decision which it has upset. I, however, think I am at liberty even as a political *detenu* to congratulate you on so signal a vindication of yourself and your recent speeches. Nevertheless I refrain, and I do so because after all our characters can best be vindicated by ourselves and our people when we stand at the bar of our conscience and of public opinion. In fact there is yet a higher, and only comparatively more infallible tribunal, but absolutely so which alone is competent to pronounce a final judgment on men and their work. To the Divine Judge who will fill the judgement seat of this august tribunal on His great Judgement Day must we leave the vindication of our characters.

Nor do I offer you congratulation on the reversal of what only too many people are apt to regard a humiliating decision. To one who has even in his old age willingly and cheerfully gone through so much pain and suffering as you have in the cause of what you held to be Truth and Justice without betraying the slightest consideration of consequences when duty dictated action and who has borne with an equal temper the smiles and the frowns of fortune the offer of congratulations at an escape from further persecution would in any case be a futility and an impertinence, and all the more so in this case when it is the Bombay High Court that deserves to be congratulated on its good sense and the vindication of Law and Justice.

*This letter was intercepted and withheld by the Deputy Commissioner. See Home Poll. Deposit, November 1916, 53, NAI.

Nevertheless I trust you will permit me to convey to you on my own behalf as well as my brother's our heartiest wishes that God may in His goodness vouchsafe to you in this the twilight of your life as wide and as long continued an opportunity as possible to serve Truth and Justice and the cause of this great but unhappy country of ours.

I must confess I had long been a pray to grave misgivings about the catholicity of your political and social ideals and the extent of the connotation of your patriotism. I confess this all the more readily today because long before today I learnt to regret those misgivings and have already offered my apologies to you in the spirit if not in the flash. It may perhaps interest you to know that what brushed these doubts and misgivings aside like so many cobwebs was your daring and the determination that you have shown in sustaining your self-respect. This may not sound as praise of your altruism, but, to my mind, in the long run it is as safe a test as any. He who would not for the world jeopardise his own self-respect would not also if he is a thinking man, permit the self-respect of the humblest of God's creatures to be placed in jeopardy however insistent may be the claims of self-aggrandisement or of the aggrandisement of his own caste, sect, community or nation. He alone is not a slave who abhors slavery in equal degree for the meanest of his fellow-beings. Your course, resolution and fortitude are an example to us younger men, whatever be our politics, and these have convinced us that after going through all this you could never contemplate with equanimity, much less desire, that even a particle of the same suffering should be inflicted on fellow-countryman, no matter of what caste or creed, equally earnest in the defence of his freedom and self-respect.

With our deepest regards as humble fellow-servants of one God and devoted fellow-workers for one Motherland.

I remain,

Sincerely and reverentially yours,
Mohamed Ali

P.S. My brother Mr. Shaukat Ali wishes me to send you his best compliments. I don't believe you have ever met him. He has met Mr. Kelkar once with me at Ahmedabad Station when I was at Baroda. Kindly remember both of us to him and thank him for us, for sending us the *Mahratta* which we enjoy greatly.

17. To Gandhi

Chhindwara
20 February 1918

My dear Mr. Gandhi,

I am a poor correspondent at best, but when the censorship came to confine my correspondence to merely private and domestic affairs I lost all zest in writing even to my most intimate friends. The weather is not in India the perennial topic of interest as it is in England, except during the rains, and then at times it becomes too tragic a subject for writing about lightly when to more than two hundred millions of our fellow-countrymen 'life is a long drawn question between a crop and a crop'. The only other topic that I can dilate upon is my health, and that too is by now as exhausted as I am myself. I have too long treated it lightly, and pretended an optimism about it that I was in fact too far from feeling, till at last I have come to acknowledge that my vitality is much reduced, and in spite of almost the caution of a hypochondriac about clods and fever, I get both far too often now to ignore altogether. But whatever else my internment may or may not have done, it has I believe set the soul free, and that compensates me for so many items on the wrong side of the account. What I could but dimly perceive before I now realise with distinctness, and it is this, that the whole aim and end of life is to serve God and obey His commandments and permit none else to share His Kingdom with Him. This seems to be too simple and commonplace an idea to have escaped one who had some pretensions to consider himself educated and cultured: and yet I confess I had never before grasped this truth in all its fullness, not regarding it as the governing idea of all life and its manifold activities. Internment made us seek refuge in the Holy Quran, and for the first time, I have to confess it, I read it through and with new eyes. It was then that this truth dawned upon me and gave me coherence and a unity to a thousand vague aspirations to do good to my people, my country and men and women in general. And, of course regimen of the soul found a new significance, and I understand, for the first time in all its clearness, what you repeat a hundred times daily, and what our Muslim mothers also taught us to repeat when tempted by Satan. 'I fear none but God. There is neither dread nor power but in God'.

*Mohamed Ali Papers, JMI.

I understand that although you think you have rightly understood the significance of the addition we had made in the form of undertaking required from us by Government last September, you want to make sure that it is so, well, I can assure you that you have interpreted it rightly, as the foregoing account of my 'conversation' would itself suggest. I regard nothing as binding upon me that is against the commands of God as conveyed in the Holy Quran and the words and acts of the Holy Prophet, on whom be God's benedictions and peace, and I declare for myself and my brother that you are at liberty to state publicly, if need be, that both of us, nevertheless believe in the British connection, and consider ourselves perfectly loyal citizens of the Empire. The so-called reservation made by me in the undertaking required by Government in particular meant that we should resist by every means at our disposal any encroachments upon the Holy Places and any interference in the question of the Khilafat and the spiritual position of the Caliph. But in this we are not taking a singular, or new and unheard of position with the malicious view of embarrassing the Government. All Muslims believe alike on these subjects, and we feal sure that there is not a single Muslim in India that cares for his salvation hereafter who would not rise against any such encroachment and any such interference in our most intimate religious beliefs and practices.

There never was any possibility of misunderstanding about this in the course of any one acquainted with universally held Muslim beliefs and universally practised Muslim observances; but if ever there was any such possibility there cannot be any after this most explicit declaration of our religious and political beliefs.

I wish you had applied again for permission to see us when we could have exchanged ideas with still greater care; and although I have given you an explicit enough assurance for both of us, we still very much wish that you could come. Do apply for permission and come. Surely the goverment cannot reasonably refuse permission to one like yourself.

Affectionate esteem from both of us and *dua* from mother. You make us jealous of her affection for you.

Yours very sincerely,
Mohamed Ali

18. To C.Y. Chintamani*

Delhi
3 September 1925

My dear Mr. Chintamani,

Am I right in believing that you are once more in your sanctum at Allahabad ? I thought of writing a few lines on the *Leader*'s 'leaderatte' in the issue of now just received, but it would not have helped to mend matters. You have done justice neither to me nor to Islam by writing in that flippant way about a religious matter, and although I know you object to 'priest in politics', meaning the spiritualisation of what is in India frequently enough mere *bagatelle* and in Europe and America only too often a means of profitering, your standing up as spokesman of the Hindu Mahasabha in the All Parties meetings at Delhi last January and the *Leader*'s anything-but-indifference to goats and cows and noisy processions, leads me to hope that you would avoid hurting the susceptibilities of non-Hindus too. As regards my speech at Lahore, why do you take the A.P.I. report as being verbatim ? If you want to know more or less exactly what I said about 'giving battle to Ibn Saud' (the A.P.I's please-not mine !) read it—if you can—in the *Hamdard* which I enclose. All I said and meant was that while *we* would risk our lives for a sacrilegious attack on the Prophet's tomb, if it *did* take place, these liars and jobbers would only pass resolutions of protest. I am no grave worshipper, but a sacrilege is a sacrilege and you know that all these disastrous Crusaders were for the possession of the tomb of one who was beloved to lie no more in it but to have raised to heaven and to be sitting on the right hand of Divine Father, being himself God too ! I write personally to you to make amends, if you care to, otherwise I would have to write in the *Comrade*.

Yours sincerely,
Mohamed Ali

*Mohamed Ali Papers, JMI.

19. M.A. Jinnah to Mohamed Ali*

Mount Pleasant Road
Malabar Hill
Bombay
30 November 1927

Dear Maulana Mohamed Ali,

We have now the final decision of Parliament with regard to the Statutory Commission. In my opinion, the principle and the policy underlying the exclusion of Indians from the Commission are proved to be more objectionable than ever.

I think you will agree with me that India is faced with a very serious crisis, and with a view to prevent individual or isolated action being taken by any prominent organisations, such as the Indian National Congress, the Muslim League, the Hindu Mahasabha and the Liberal Federation, it is essential that a policy of common and concerted action should be adopted if we are to meet with my succees.

I have already received the assurance of the President of the Indian National Congress that Congress leaders would be willing to come to Bombay between the 12th and 15th of December. I have every hope that leaders of the Liberal Federation will also attend. I therefore earnestly expect you to let me know *by wire* that you will come for certain, so that I can give the assurance to the leaders of the Congress, the Liberal Federation, the Muslim League, the Hindu Sabha and the Indian Merchants Chamber.

I think the occasion is one which requires your presence at any cost of personal comfort or convenience. I therefore trust that you will not fail to come. It is only by adopting a common policy and programme of action that we can succeed, and this conference will strengthen the hands of the leaders of the different organisations which are meeting during the Xmas week, in guiding and shaping the policies of their respective bodies. I may add that the leaders of these organisations are most likely to attend.

Your presence will be absolutely necessary to complete the representative character of the conference.

Yours sincerely,
M.A. Jinnah

*Mohamed Ali Papers, JMI.

20 To M.A. Jinnah*

Khilafat House
Love Lane
Bombay
26 December 1928

My dear Jinnah,

The friends that you wanted us to bring to the League have after the most careful consideration decided that no useful purpose will be served by their coming to the League meetings unless you can protect the minorities from being swamped by the majorities in the mixed electorates in the manner suggested by the Bihar Muslim All Parties Cnoference—a Federal system of Government is accepted in addition to your own amendment and the amendment you suggested that I should move for the Punjab and Bengal and the amendment about Sind separation for the removal of the Nehru Committee provision. We all would love to help you, but this is the farthest we can.

Yours sincerely,
Mohamed Ali

*Courtesy : Mr. Rafique Akhtar, East and West Publishing Co., Karachi.

21. To M.A. Jinnah*

Iqbal Manzil
Karol Bagh
Delhi
16 January 1930

My dear Jinnah,

I received your letter of the 7th instant on the tenth, but have been unable to write back earlier as my eyes have been giving me great trouble and even now that I am writing, I am more than half blind and am disobeying my doctor's orders.

I am sorry that the Liberals and the Congress have parted company so soon, but I am not surprised. As for the Muslims my advice to them is not to close the door of negotiations on government or any party, and to examine every scheme with a view to satisfy themselves that

1 We are really getting freedom, or Swaraj, or full responsible government, whether with or without the British connection—by whatever name people call it, and that
2 The Muslims are getting an adequate and effective share in the governance of India as defined in the points which you and we formulated last year.

As you are aware, bitter experience of the British, both in India and in Great Britain had driven us in 1927 to the painful conclusion that they did not mean to give freedom or Swaraj or full responsible government to India, and at Madras we declared Independence to be our goal. We stuck to that at Calcutta last year even when the Congress and the Liberals accepted Dominion Status in the Convention in spite of my solitary opposition and the demurring of Srinivasa Iyengar and his party. Nevertheless I was sufficiently impressed by the Viceroy's announcement to believe that a change of heart was at long last taking place, and I was willing to take part, if invited, in the Round Table Conference in order to examine what the British proposed to give us, provided that my community was truly and adequately represented therein.

*Courtesy: Mr. Rafique Akhtar, East and West Publishing Co., Karachi.

I refused to go so far as the Congress and Liberal leaders were going at Delhi, and I think I was wiser, for the two have parted company on the 23rd December last, which they should not have done after their agreement on the 2nd November. It now appears that the Congress leaders would participate in the Conference *only if* the *immediate* grant of Dominion Status is assured and would not go to press their case for it as they should do; and I *fear* that the Liberal leaders would go even if they are assured that Dominion Status would *not immediately* be *granted* and would accept something less, like provincial autonomy, and dyarchy in the Central Government. Such disagreements should have been unthinkable if both parties had laid their cards on the table on the 1st November. Now, I am prepared to take part in any conference with a view to examine what is proposed for the nation and what is proposed for my community. But while I am *not* committed to a refusal of *Dominion Status* at once, I can not commit myself to an abhorrence of *Independence* either. This is very important, and I understand that Nawab Ismail Khan, who presided over the Khilafat Conference at Lahore, has informed you that while we have not made the attainment of complete Independence our *creed* like the Congress, we have reiterated that it is still our goal as it was in 1927 and 1928. We therefore do *not exclude* those who want only Dominion Status, as the Congress must do henceforward. But we do *not exclude* those either who want Independence. For my part I am prepared to *accept* Dominion Status; but I am not going to make that my goal to be attained 'in due course'. The Great War gave us two new words 'Defeatism' and 'Camouflage'. I attacked the Defeatism of the Congress last year; but I shall not reconcile myself to the 'Camouflage' of the Liberals or the British this year.

For my part I do not close the door of negotiations on any party, official or non-official, Hindu or Muslim. But I would like that door to remain open, if I am invited to enter by it. Do not close it after I have come in and say 'You are now committed to the attainment of *Dominion Status*'.

I have placed my views fully and frankly before you and you can communicate them to any one you like. If the Conference remains open in the sense I have explained, I shall gladly take part in it and if Shaukat and you think that his name and mine among those issuing the invitation will serve any useful purpose, I have no objection. But perhaps Ismail is right and it would be better that we should merely be guests and not among the hosts. Kindly show this letter to Shaukat as it is too much for me to write another.

With my best wishes for the year,

Your sincerely,
Mohamed Ali

22. T.B. Sapru to Mohamed Ali*

19 Albert Road
Allahabad
15 January 1930

Dear Maulana Mohamed Ali,

I venture to approach you with request that you may kindly approve of the idea which is strongly entertained in many circles that having regard to the present situation all those, who are committed to, or favour the Dominion Status programme, should meet on a common platform to focus and express opinion on the subject. It is intended to call an All-Parties Conference of what I may call the Dominion Status School of politicians sometime in February next at Delhi. It is realised that one of the most essential conditions of our success is a satisfactory settlement of the communal issue, and it is hoped that if each party approaches the question in a spirit of give and take, reasonable settlement is by no means improbable. Further if we can come to such a settlement—as I hope we shall be able to do—we should apply ourselves to the preparation of our case in view of the Round Table Conference to be held in London. For the present I am only anxious to know whether you favour the proposal relating to the holding of an All-Parties Conference, and if so, whether you will be good enough to be a signatory to the invitation to be issued. I may point out to you that it is not intended that any single party should take the lead in this matter but that all parties should unite in convening this Conference, nor is it intended that there should be a merger

*Mohamed Ali Papers, JMI.

of parties. What is aimed at is that while each party may retain its individuality and continue to work according to its constitution, all may meet together on a common platform for the purposes indicated above. Questions of controversial character must be left over for discussion and settlement at the contemplated Delhi Conference.

I shall suggest that if you agree you may kindly write to me not only in your personal capacity but as representing your party.

I shall esteem it a great favour if you will kindly let me have an early reply.

Yours sincerely,
T.B. Sapru

23. T.B. Sapru to Mohamed Ali*

19 Albert Road
Allahabad
4 February 1930

My dear Maulana Mohamed Ali,

I have written to Maulvi Shafi Daudi, Sir Mohammad Shafi and Mr. Jinnah and am writing to you also now to kindly take steps to select your representatives for the preliminary conference which was agreed to during our interview. I am suggesting the afternoon of the 26th or 27th February for this meeting at Delhi. I have no doubt that Mr. Jinnah has already told you that the representatives of the Hindu Sabha whom I met also were agreed to come to this preliminary conference. May I personally thank you for the courteous manner in which you were good enough to discuss outstanding questions with me at Delhi.

With kind regards,

Yours sincerely,
T.B. Sapru

*Sapru Papers, vol. 38 (II series), p. 185, National Library, Calcutta. I am grateful to the family of the late Sir Tej Bahadur Sapru for allowing me access to the papers. The late Dr. Tara Chand was good enough to write to the family on my behalf.

24. To T.B. Sapru*

15 April 1930

[Telegram]

Have telegraphed Viceroy begins I earnestly appeal to your excellency not to permit situation to become graver by arrest of Mahatma Gandhi stop both he and government have made sufficient demonstration of their strength stop I pray consideration of prestige will prevent neither from seeking rapprochement by retracing their steps and bringing about peace and freedom stop with an assurance from you we shall try our utmost to bring about peace honourable to both stop I am telegraphing this to Mahatmaji also and similarly appealing to him ends please join me in this appeal and wire to both immediate holding of your committee meeting at Bombay absolutely essential please wire Patro wire reply all points.

Mohamed Ali

*Sapru Papers, vol. 38 (II series), p. 201.

25. To the Earl of Halifax*

Camp Bhopal
11 September 1930

Your Excellency,

I thank you for kindly conveying to me the invitation of His Majesty's Government to the Round Table Conference which is to meet for the solution of the constitutional problem of India.

Believing as I did in the freedom of every person, community and country as their birth-right, I was naturally greatly dissatisfied with the denial of this right through the system of Government which had been established in India, and sought like those associated with me to win back our freedom if possible with the British connection and if necessary without it.

The bitter experience of the past led us to conclude that the representatives of the British nation and the officials employed in India did not really intend to restore to us our birth-right, and three years ago we resolved to win back freedom and made complete independence our goal.

However, Your Excellency's visit to England last year and the announcement which you made on your return gave us hope once more that our freedom could be won while still retaining the British connection. Although there have been symptoms indicating that no Government would retain the confidence of the politically minded people in Britain if it resolved to do justice to India and restore to us our birth-right of freedom, I most gratefully acknowledge, if I may say so, that I have been deeply impressed by your personal desire to be just and fair to us and there have been other indications also that you have been able at last to induce some others as well in your country to share your goodwill towards us and your righteous intentions.

Therefore I resolved with many of my associates not to slam the door of negotiations that Your Excellency's statement of 31st October 1930 had opened and we are still adhering to that resolu-

*Mohamed Ali Papers, JMI.

tion. In fact it was our efforts that saved the Muslims from being misled into joining the present Civil Disobedience movement.

While I deny the right of any but Indians themselves to shape their destinies, I am not only willing but anxious to proceed to England, along with other representatives of Indian communities, parties and interests to confer with the representatives of Great Britain and persuade them to recognise India's natural demand for self-determination.

I do not yet know authoritatively who will be the other delegates from India which the Government has selected. But I trust that all India including my own community would be truly represented and with this confidence I gratefully accept the very kind invitation of His Majesty's Government.

I trust I shall be able to assist the Conference in understanding the full connotation of the word 'self' in the expression self-determination and that an agreed scheme of constitution for a responsible Government for a free India would be framed as the result of our labours in which while we rid ourselves of the foreign incubus that has troubled us so long we shall not create for ourselves a home made incubus of certain small monopolist castes and interests pretending to speak in the name of the majority in India and claiming to control the affairs and destinies of the entire Indian nation.

As Your Excellency is probably aware I am not really in a fit condition to undertake so long a journey to a cold country at a time when its climate would be far from agreeable and to do constant work from day to day some of which would no doubt produce at times excitement most dangerous to one like myself suffering from a dilated heart, and practically still confined to bed. My left eye had become hopelessly blind sometime ago and now the right eye too is so seriously affected that reading and writing are impossible and any further strain may make me completely blind. But when so serious an attempt is to be made to shape the destinies of my country and community, I cannot resist the yearning of my heart to deliver to those attempting this task the message with which I feel I have heen charged and it is only on this account that I hope to proceed to London along with my wife and brother in spite of the obvious danger that every doctor has told me I shall be running. I hope even a sick man's labours may prove of some slight use.

I trust that in consideration of my health such facilities as a sick man and his relations nursing him need, will not be denied.

Thanking your Excellency once more,

I remain,
Yours sincerely,
Mohamed Ali

BIBLIOGRAPHY

UNPUBLISHED SOURCES

Private Papers

Aligarh Muslim University Archives, Aligarh

Papers relating to the Non-cooperation movement at M.A.O. College, Aligarh.

India Office Library, London [IOL]

Harcourt Butler Papers	MSS.	EUR.	F.	116
Chelmsford Papers	MSS.	EUR.	E.	264
Hailey Papers	MSS.	EUR.	E.	220
Irwin Papers	MSS.	EUR.	C.	152
Meston Papers	MSS.	EUR.	F.	136
Montagu Papers	MSS.	EUR.	D.	523
Reading Papers	MSS.	EUR.	E.	238
Sykes Papers	MSS.	EUR.	F.	150
Willingdon Papers	MSS.	EUR.	F.	93

National Archives of India, New Delhi

G.K. Gokhale Papers (F. No. 341).

National Library, Calcutta

Sapru Papers

Nehru Memorial Museum and Library

All-India Congress Committee Papers
Brelvi Papers
Daryabadi Papers
Khwaja Papers
Motilal Nehru Papers

University Library, Cambridge

Crewe Papers
Hardinge Papers

Jamia Millia Islamia, New Delhi

Ansari Papers
Mohamed Ali Papers
Shaukat Ali Papers

Centre of South Asian Studies, Cambridge

R.E. Hawkins Papers
A.P. Hume Papers
J.C. Curry Papers

Government Records

National Archives of India, New Delhi [NAI]

Records of the Home Department of the Government of India, filed as Home Political. Home Political files are divided into A, B and D (Deposit) categories.

PUBLISHED SOURCES

Newspapers and Journals

English

Bengalee (Calcutta).*
Bombay Chronicle (Bombay).*
Comrade (Calcutta and Delhi), Jamia Millia Islamia, New Delhi.
Indian Annual Register, 1923-32 (Calcutta), published as the *Indian Quarterly Register, 1924-29.*
Leader (Allahabad).*
Mahratta (Poona).*
Mussalman (Calcutta).
Moslem Outlook (Calcutta).*
Searchlight (Patna).*
Times of India (Bombay).*
Tribune (Lahore).*

*Consulted only isolated issues.

Urdu

Aligarh Magazine (Aligarh), Special Number: Aligarh Number 1953-55.

A'aj Kal (Delhi), Publications Division, 1978.

Aligarh Magazine, Department of Urdu, Aligarh Muslim University 1960-61.

Hamdard (Delhi).

Jamia (Delhi), Mohamed Ali Number, 1980

Nigar (Karachi), *Maulana Mohamed Ali Jauhar Sadi Conference*, 1978.

Nuqqush (Lahore), *Makatib Number*, 1957.

Published Books, Articles and Unpublished Theses

Adhikari, G. (ed.) *Documents of the History of the Communist Party of India, 1923-1925* (Delhi, 1974).

Azad, A.K. *India Wins Freedom: An Autobiographical Narrative* (Bombay, 1959).

Bamford, P.C. *Histories of the Khilafat and Non-cooperation Movements* (Delhi, 1975 Reprint).

Brass, P. *Language Religion and Politics in North India* (Cambridge, 1974).

Brown, J.M. *Gandhi's Rise to Power: Indian Politics 1915-1922* (Cambridge, 1972).

——— *Gandhi and Civil Disobedience: The Mahatma in Indian Politics, 1928-1934* (Cambridge, 1977).

Desai, M. (ed.) *Day-To-Day with Gandhi* (Varanasi, 1968).

Daryabadi, A.M. *Maqalat-i-Majid* (Bombay, n.d.).

——— *Mohamed Ali : Za'ati Diary ke chund Auraq*, (Hyderabad, 1943).

Datta, V.N. and B. Cleghorn (eds.) *A Nationalist Muslim and Indian Politics: Being the selected correspondence of the late Dr. Syed Mahmud* (Delhi, 1974).

Edib, H. *The Conflict of East and West in Turkey* (Delhi, 1935).

Faruqi, Z.H. *The Deoband School and the Demand for Pakistan* (Bombay, 1963).

Furbank, P.N. *E.M. Forster A Life: The Growth of the Novelist 1879-1914* (London, 1978).

Gopal, Ram. *Indian Muslims: A Political History* (Bombay, 1959).

Gandhi, M.K. *Collected Works of Mahatma Gandhi* (Delhi, in process of publication).

Haq, A. *Chand Hum Aasr* (Karachi, 1952 edn.).

Haq, M. (ed.) *Mohamed Ali : Life and Work* (Karachi, 1978.)

Hamid, *A Muslim Separatism in India : A brief Survey 1858-1947* (Karachi, 1971 edn).

Hardy, P. *The Muslims of British India* (Cambridge, 1972).

———— *Partners in Freedom—and True Muslims : The Political thought of some Muslim scholars in British India, 1912-1947* (Scandinavian Institute of Asian studies, 1971).

Hassan, Mohibbul 'Mahatma Gandhi and the Indian Muslims' in S.C. Biswas (ed.), *Gandhi Theory and Practice : Social Impact and Contemporary Relevance* (Simla, 1969).

Hasan, Mushirul (ed.) *Communal and Pan-Islamic Trends in Colonial India* (Delhi, 1981).

———— 'Religion and Politics : The ulama and the Khilafat Movement', *Economic and Political Weekly*, 16 May 1981.

———— *Nationalism and Communal Politics in India, 1916-1928* (Delhi, 1979).

——— (ed.) *Muslims and the Congress: Select Correspondence of M.A. Ansari, 1912-1935* (Delhi, 1979).

Heyde, U. *Foundations of Turkish Nationalism : The Life and Teachings of Ziya Golp* (London, 1950).

Husain, A. *Fazl-i-Husain: A Political Biography* (Bombay, 1946).

Iqbal, A. *Life and Times of Mohamed Ali* (Delhi, 1978 Reprint).

——— (ed.) *My Life A Fragment : An Autobiographical Sketch of Maulana Mohamed Ali* (Lahore, 1946)

——— (ed.) *Select Writings and Speeches of Maulana Mohamed Ali* (Lahore, 1944).

Jafri, Rais Ahmad, *Sirat-i-Muhammad Ali* (Delhi, 1932).

——— (ed.) *Maktubat-i-Muhammad Ali* (Hyderabad, 1945).

——— (ed.) *Ifadat-i-Mohamed Ali* (Hyderabad, n.d.).

——— (ed.) *Selections from Mohamed Ali's Comrade* (Lahore, 1965).

Jagadisan (ed.) *Letters of V.S. Srinivasa Sastri* (Asia Publishing House, 1963).

Jain, M.S. *The Aligarh Movement : Its origin and Development* (Agra, 1965).

Khaliquzzaman, C. *Pathway to Pakistan* (Lahore, 1961).

Kumar, R. (ed.) *Essays on Gandhian Politics: The Rowlatt Satyagraha of 1919* (Oxford, 1971).

Lelyveld, D. *Aligarh's First Generation: Muslim Solidarity in British India* (Princeton University Press, 1978).

———— 'Three Aligarh Students: Aftab Ahmad Khan, Ziauddin Ahmad and Muhammad Ali', *Modern Asian Studies*, VIII, 1974.

Low, D.A. (ed.) *Congress and the Raj* (London, 1977).

Malhotra, N. 'The Khilafat Movement in Delhi: A socio-political study of Delhi Muslims 1912-1927'. (Unpublished M. Phil thesis, Delhi University, 1981).

Mcpherson, K. *The Muslim Microcoihlm: Calcutta, 1918-1935* (Wiesbaden, 1974).

Minault, G. 'The Khilafat Movement: A Study of Indian Muslim Leadership 1919-1924', (Unpublished Ph.D. thesis, Pennsylvania, 1972).

——— & D. Lelyveld 'The Campaign for a Muslim University', *Modern Asian Studies*, vol. 8, 1974.

Muhammad, S. *Freedom Movement in India: The Role of Ali Brothers* (Delhi, 1979).

——— (ed.) *Unpublished Letters of the Ali Brothers* (Delhi, 1979).

Mujeeb, M. *The Indian Muslims* (London, 1967).

Nehru, J. *A Bunch of Old Letters* (Bombay, 1966 edn.).

———— *An Autobiography* (London, 1936).

Pandey, G. *The Ascendancy of the Congress in Uttar Pradesh 1928-1934: A Study in Imperfect Mobilization* (Delhi, 1978).

Qureshi, I.H. *The Muslim Community of the Indo-Pakistan Sub-continent, 610-1947: A Brief Historical Analysis* (The Hague, 1962).

———— *Ulema in Politics: A Study relating to the political activities of the ulema in the South-Asian Subcontinent from 1556 to 1947* (Karachi, 1974).

Rahman, M. *From Consultation to Confrontation: A Study of the Muslim League in British Indian Politics 1906-1912* (London, 1970).

Robinson, F. *Separatism Among Indian Muslims: The Politics of the United Provinces' Muslims, 1860-1923* (Cambridge, 1974).

Sarwar, M. (ed.) *Mazameen-i-Mohamed Ali*, 2 vols. (Delhi, 1938).

——— (ed.) *Khutut-i-Mohamed Ali* (Delhi, 1940).

——— (ed.) *Mohamed Ali Ke Europe Ka Safar* (Lahore, 1941).
Schimmel, A. *Gabriel's Wing : A Study into the Religious Ideas of Sir Muhammad Iqbal* (Leiden, 1973).
Shahjahanpuri, A.S. (ed.) *Siyasi Maktubat Rais-ul-Ahrar* (Karachi, 1978).
——— (ed.) *Maulana Mohamed Ali: Sawanah wa Khidmat* (Karachi, n.d.).
Shakir, M. *Khilafat to Partition* (Delhi, 1972).
Siddiqi, A. *Iqbal: Jadugar-i-Hindi Nizad* (Delhi, 1980).
Spear, P. *India Remembered* (Delhi, 1981).
Smith, W.C. *Modern Islam in India* (London, 1946).
Wasti, S.R. *Lord Minto and the Indian Nationalist Movement, 1905-1910* (Oxford, 1964).
Watson, W.J. 'Muhammad Ali and the Khilafat Movement', (Unpublished M.A. thesis, McGill University, 1955).
Zubayri, M.A. *Hayat-i-Muhsin* (Aligarh, 1934).

INDEX

SHEIKH ABDUL KARIM,
B. A. (*Alig:*) Gold-Medallist,
LL. B. Vakil.
High Court Lahore.

Lyallpur,

Dated 21st Nov. 1920

Dear Sir,

I have already been in touch with the events at Aligarh & you would remember that I sent a wire on the 18th of October & later when the meeting of the Trustees was to take place on the 27th of the last month. There can be no doubt that the Trustees arrived at a very right decision & saved the institution from the baneful influence of the non-cooperation propaganda. Although I am, in this respect, mostly blaming the <u>Ulemas</u> who are giving <u>fatwas</u> supporting the item of non-cooperation movement promulgated by Mr Gandhi & his colleagues I find that the majority of Mussalmans, without thinking over the consequences which will ensue to our Community, [illegible] are becoming followers of this movement.

Nothing could have been better under the then circumstances for you than to close the College, & there is no doubt that it would prove a very salutary step in the interests of the College but there is one thing which is troubling me still, & which I have to respectfully suggest that as long as Mr Mohammad Ali stays in Aligarh, there will not be an end to the trouble. His free access to the College mosque & his free mixing with the students when they return to the College when he would instil into them his own ideas which are not in any way beneficial to our Community would be a constant source of disturbance & while you would, I have no doubt, be able to stop his ingress into the mosque which forms part of the College buildings, it would be more advisable